Company's Coming®

SOUPS & SANDWICHES

by
Jean Paré

companyscoming.com
↖ visit our web-site

Dedication

Enjoy the adventure of a new twist on an old theme.
Soups and sandwiches—a family tradition in the making.

Cover Photo

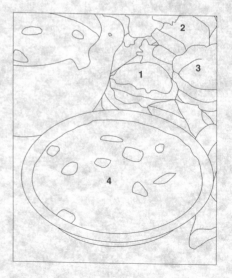

SOUPS & SANDWICHES

Copyright © Company's Coming Publishing Limited
All Rights Reserved

Twenty-third Printing January 2003

Canadian Cataloguing in Publication Data

Paré, Jean
Soups & sandwiches

Includes index.
ISBN 0-9690695-6-1

1. Soups. 2.Sandwiches. I. Title. II. Title: Soups and sandwiches

TX757.P37 1998   641.8'13   C98-900156-3

Published and Distributed by
Company's Coming Publishing Limited
2311 - 96 Street
Edmonton, Alberta, Canada T6N 1G3
www.companyscoming.com

**Published Simultaneously in
Canada and the United States of America**

Printed In Canada

Company's Coming Cookbook Series

Quick & easy recipes, everyday ingredients!

Original Series
- Softcover, 160 pages
- 6" x 9" (15 cm x 23 cm) format
- Lay-flat binding
- Full colour photos
- Nutrition information

Greatest Hits Series
- Softcover, 106 & 124 pages
- 8" x 9 9/16" (20 cm x 24 cm) format
- Paperback binding
- Full colour photos
- Nutrition information

Lifestyle Series
- Softcover, 160 pages
- 8" x 10" (20 cm x 25 cm) format
- Paperback & spiral binding
- Full colour photos
- Nutrition information

Special Occasion Series
- Hardcover & softcover, 192 pages
- 8 1/2" x 11" (22 cm x 28 cm) format
- Durable sewn binding
- Full colour throughout
- Nutrition information

See page 157
for a complete listing
of __all__ cookbooks
or visit
companyscoming.com

table of Contents

the Jean Paré story

Jean Paré grew up understanding that the combination of family, friends and home cooking is the essence of a good life. From her mother she learned to appreciate good cooking, while her father praised even her earliest attempts. When she left home she took with her many acquired family recipes, her love of cooking and her intriguing desire to read recipe books like novels!

In 1963, when her four children had all reached school age, Jean volunteered to cater to the 50th anniversary of the Vermilion School of Agriculture, now Lakeland College. Working out of her home, Jean prepared a dinner for over 1000 people which launched a flourishing catering operation that continued for over eighteen years. During that time she was provided with countless opportunities to test new ideas with immediate feedback—resulting in empty plates and contented customers! Whether preparing cocktail sandwiches for a house party or serving a hot meal for 1500 people, Jean Paré earned a reputation for good food, courteous service and reasonable prices.

"Why don't you write a cookbook?" Time and again, as requests for her recipes mounted, Jean was asked that question. Jean's response was to team up with her son, Grant Lovig, in the fall of 1980 to form Company's Coming Publishing Limited. April 14, 1981, marked the debut of "150 DELICIOUS SQUARES", the first Company's Coming cookbook in what soon would become Canada's most popular cookbook series.

Jean Paré's operation has grown steadily from the early days of working out of a spare bedroom in her home. Full-time staff includes marketing personnel located in major cities across Canada. Home Office is based in Edmonton, Alberta in a modern building constructed specially for the company.

Today the company distributes throughout Canada and the United States in addition to numerous overseas markets, all under the guidance of Jean's daughter, Gail Lovig. Best-sellers many times over in English, Company's Coming cookbooks have also been published published in French and Spanish. Familiar and trusted in home kitchens around the world, Company's Coming cookbooks are offered in a variety of formats, including the original softcover series.

Jean Paré's approach to cooking has always called for quick and easy recipes using everyday ingredients. Even when travelling, she is constantly on the lookout for new ideas to share with her readers. At home, she can usually be found researching and writing recipes, or working in the company's test kitchen. Jean continues to gain new supporters by adhering to what she calls "the golden rule of cooking": never share a recipe you wouldn't use yourself. It's an approach that works—*millions of times over!*

Foreword

Nutritious soup may precede a meal as an appetizer, may be a substantial meal in itself, or may be the grand finale after an outing.

Stocks made from scratch are excellent for soup base. Quick and easy stock recipes are also included in this book. A richer flavored soup will result if you replace some of the milk in a recipe with cream.

Serve soup either hot or cold—never warm. Choose hot Apple Broth or Cold Cantaloupe soup for tasty interesting appetizers. In the heat of summer cold soup is perfect in small portions for lunch or dinner.

Delicious and filling hot soups such as Tuna Bisque, Pepper Pot or Corn soup may stand alone as a complete meal. After a cool outing serve a warming lunch such as Beef Barley Soup, Fresh Pea Soup or Split Pea Turkey Soup. In a hurry? Try a convenience soup such as Rush Asparagus or Quick Broccoli Soup.

Most soups freeze well. Cubed vegetables tend to go mealy, especially potatoes. Better results are obtained when vegetables are shredded.

Sandwiches are a natural addition to serve with soup. Hot or cold, simple, hearty or robust, sandwiches round out any nutritious meal. Add new flair to everyday sandwiches by cutting them in various shapes and sizes. Try making old standby favorites with bagels, Kaiser rolls, poppy seed buns, onion buns and small loaf-type buns. A large selection of fillings and spreads are included for interesting and easy sandwich fixings. Try Jelly Roll Bread, Pizza Buns or Pita Sandwiches.

Although mayonnaise is recommended consistently throughout this book, it may be interchanged with salad dressing.

All sandwiches may be frozen successfully, although it is not recommended to freeze fillings containing mayonnaise or salad dressing.

In the warmth of summer or the cool of winter, create a sensation with soups and sandwiches. It will become a family tradition—honest to goodness!

Jean Paré

Fun biscuits to serve with any soup. Serve right from the oven and you have hot lips!

All-purpose flour	2 cups	500 mL
Baking powder	4 tsp.	25 mL
Granulated sugar	2 tbsp.	30 mL
Salt	1 tsp.	5 mL
Butter or margarine, cold	1/3 cup	100 mL
Milk, cold	3/4 cup	225 mL

Butter or margarine to spread

Mix first 4 ingredients together in bowl. Cut in butter until crumbly.

Add milk. Stir with fork until it forms a ball. Add a bit more milk if necessary to make a soft dough. Knead 10 times on lightly floured surface. Roll ¼ inch (6 mm) thick. Cut into 2¾ inch (7 cm) circles. Cut through center of each with sharp knife to barely score surface. Spread with butter. Fold over (butter inside) and press edges together. Arrange on greased baking sheet. Bake in 425°F (220°C) oven for about 8 to 10 minutes or until risen and nicely browned. Makes about 20.

Pictured on page 17.

SNUGGLY DOGS: Roll dough ¼ inch (6 mm) thick. Cut into 12 rectangles. Completely enclose wiener that has been heated and wiped dry. Press dampened edges of dough to seal. You may want to dab a bit of mustard along side of wiener. Try rolling 1 cheese slice around meat before enclosing. Arrange on greased baking sheet. Bake in 425°F (220°C) oven for about 10 minutes until browned. Serve hot. Makes 12.

Pictured on page 89.

If a cannibal ate his mother's sister, he would be an aunt eater.

BREAD STICKS

Keep a package of refrigerated biscuits on hand to turn these out in no time.

Refrigerated biscuits - pkg. of 10	1	1
Milk		
Sesame seed	1 tbsp.	15 mL
Seasoned salt	1 tbsp.	15 mL
Dill seed	1 tbsp.	15 mL

Separate biscuits and cut in half. Roll on lightly floured surface to make pencil-shape about 4 inches (10 cm) long.

Brush with milk. Roll some in sesame seed, some in seasoned salt, and some in dill seed. Place on greased baking sheet. Bake in 400°F (200°C) oven until browned, about 7 to 10 minutes. Makes 20.

Pictured on page 53.

FORCEMEAT BALLS

Tasty little morsels that give an unusual interest to soup, especially a broth-type.

Egg	1	1
Dry bread crumbs	1/3 cup	75 mL
Butter or margarine, softened	1 tbsp.	15 mL
Parsley flakes	1/2 tsp.	2 mL
Salt	1/2 tsp.	2 mL
Pepper	1/4 tsp.	1 mL
Flour to coat		

Beat egg with spoon in small bowl. Stir in remaining ingredients. Shape into tiny marble size balls. If this is too soft to work with, add a few more crumbs. Coat each ball with flour. Drop into soup. Boil for about 5 minutes. Makes 8 to 10.

MARINATED ONION RINGS

Keep a container full of these in the refrigerator. Always ready to add to your favorite sandwich or to serve on the side.

Large Spanish onion, sliced in thin rings	1	1
Cold water to cover, approximately	12 cups	3 L
Granulated sugar	1 cup	250 mL
Vinegar	1 cup	250 mL
Water	1 cup	250 mL
Cooking oil	1 tbsp.	15 mL

Slice peeled onion as thinly as possible. A food slicer makes this a snap to do. Separate into rings and place in bowl. Cover with lots of water. Let stand for 1 hour.

In small saucepan mix sugar, vinegar, water and oil. Heat and stir until sugar dissolves. Drain onions. Pour sugar-vinegar mixture over onions. Let stand in refrigerator, covered, for at least 1 day before serving.

PASTA DUMPLINGS

Adds interest to broth-type soups.

Eggs	2	2
All-purpose flour	1 cup	250 mL
Milk	1/4 cup	60 mL
Salt	1/4 tsp.	1 mL

Beat eggs slightly with spoon in small bowl. Add flour, milk and salt. Mix together. Drop tiny bits, about 1/2 tsp. (2 mL) each into simmering soup. Cover and simmer for 10 minutes. Makes 6 dozen.

SOUP GARNISHES

Makes a special presentation.

PUFFED LIDS: Roll puff pastry to fit ovenproof soup bowl, allowing enough to be pressed onto top outside edge of bowl. Bake in 400°F (200°C) oven for about 20 minutes until browned. Try on French Onion Soup, page 79, Tomato Soup Au Gratin, page 73, or any of your choice.

CROUTON PUFFS: Roll puff pastry ⅛ inch (5 mm) thick. Cut into small circles or other shapes. Bake in 375°F (190°C) oven until browned. Sprinkle puffs on soup just before serving.

RYE BREAD

A no-yeast loaf that fills the air with a great aroma as it bakes. Good with soup.

Rye flour	2½ cups	625 mL
All-purpose flour	1 cup	250 mL
Baking powder	2 tsp.	10 mL
Baking soda	1 tsp.	5 mL
Egg	1	1
Mild molasses	½ cup	125 mL
Sour milk - 1 tbsp. (15 mL) vinegar plus milk	1¼ cups	300 mL

Mix first 4 dry ingredients together in bowl.

Beat egg with spoon in another bowl. Add molasses and sour milk. Mix and add to dry ingredients. Stir to mix. Scrape into a greased 9 × 5 inch (23 × 13 cm) pan. Bake in 350°F (180°C) oven for 45 minutes or until an inserted toothpick comes out clean. Remove from pan. Cool on rack. Makes 1 loaf.

CRANBERRY BISCUITS

Turn a package of biscuits into a quick soup accompaniment.

Refrigerated biscuits - pkg. of 10	1	1
Cranberry sauce	²/₃ cup	150 mL

Grease medium sized muffin tin. Put 1 tbsp. (15 mL) cranberry sauce in each cup. Place biscuit into each cup. Bake in 425°F (220°C) oven for about 10 minutes or until browned. Serve with poultry soups. Makes 10 biscuits.

QUICK BROCCOLI SOUP

Makes a fast soup from the shelf.

Frozen chopped broccoli	10 oz.	284 mL
Water	1 cup	250 mL
Condensed cream of mushroom soup	10 oz.	284 mL
Milk	1¼ cups	284 mL
Butter or margarine	2 tbsp.	30 mL
Salt	½ tsp.	2 mL
Pepper	⅛ tsp.	0.5 mL
Cheddar cheese for garnish		

Cook broccoli in water. Do not drain.

Add remaining ingredients and simmer 3 or 4 minutes. Soup may be served as is, may be run through the blender, or may have some cheese added. If served as is, garnish with grated Cheddar cheese. Makes about 3½ cups (800 mL). Pictured on page 71.

QUICK ONION SOUP

Gourmet soup from a can. Streamlined.

Condensed onion soup	10 oz.	284 mL
Condensed beef broth	10 oz.	284 mL
Thinly sliced onion, in short lengths	½ cup	125 mL
Butter or margarine	2 tsp.	10 mL
French bread slices (or croutons)		
Parmesan cheese or Mozzarella		

Put soup and broth into saucepan to heat slowly.

Meanwhile, brown onion in butter, stirring often until a rich brown color. Add to soup and broth mixture. Heat. Divide among oven proof bowls. Top with toasted bread slices or croutons. Cover with lots of cheese. Heat in 400°F (200°C) oven to melt cheese or broil. Makes about 5 cups (1.1 L).

Note: If bowls aren't ovenproof or broiler-proof, broil cheese-covered toast separately and add to soup before serving.

EASIEST ONION SOUP: Heat 10 oz. (284 mL) condensed onion soup with 1¼ cups (284 mL) water. Cover as above or with Puffed Lids, page 12.

LOBSTER BISQUE

A snap to make. For a special event, use heavy cream instead of light. Nice texture and color. Good appetizer.

Condensed tomato soup	10 oz.	284 mL
Condensed cream of mushroom soup	10 oz.	284 mL
Milk	1¼ cups	284 mL
Light cream	1¼ cups	284 mL
Canned lobster, cartilage removed	5 oz.	142 g

Run all ingredients through blender. Transfer to saucepan. Heat to serve. Makes about 6½ cups (1.5 L).

CRAB BISQUE A LA VI

A very special soup in no time flat. Can't be purchased from a store. Good with or without curry and sherry.

Condensed cream of asparagus soup	10 oz.	284 mL
Condensed cream of mushroom soup	10 oz.	284 mL
Canned crab, cartilage removed	5 oz.	142 g
Milk	½ cup	125 mL
Cereal cream	½ cup	125 mL
Curry powder (optional)	½ tsp.	2 mL
Sherry (optional)	1 - 2 tbsp.	15 - 30 mL
Croutons or Cheddar cheese for garnish		

Put first 6 ingredients into saucepan. Heat to just below the boiling point.

Stir in sherry to taste. Garnish with croutons or a bit of grated Cheddar cheese. Makes about 4 cups (1 L).

LOBSTER BISQUE A LA VI: Omit crab. Add 5 oz. (142 g) canned lobster, cartilage removed. A great way to spread lobster to serve 4 to 6 people.

QUICK SPINACH SOUP

Made from shelf and freezer, this is creamy-good.

Condensed cream of chicken soup	20 oz.	568 mL
Milk	2½ cups	568 mL
Frozen chopped spinach, thawed and squeezed dry	10 oz.	284 mL
Salt	½ tsp.	2 mL
Pepper	⅛ tsp.	0.5 mL
Lemon juice	½ tsp.	2 mL

Combine all together in large saucepan. Bring to boil. Simmer about 5 minutes. Serve as is or run through blender to desired state of smoothness. Makes a generous 4 cups (1 L).

CHICKEN CURRY SOUP

Different and mild. Made from supplies on your shelf.

Butter or margarine	2 tbsp.	30 mL
Chopped onion	1 cup	250 mL
Curry powder	³/₄ tsp.	4 mL
Water	1 cup	250 mL
Chicken bouillon cubes - ¹/₅ oz. (6 g) size	2	2
Condensed cream of celery soup	10 oz.	284 mL
Canned tomatoes, drained and broken up	14 oz.	398 mL
Canned flaked chicken	5 oz.	142 g
Light cream or milk	1 cup	250 mL
Chives, parsley or croutons for garnish		

Put butter, onion and curry powder in saucepan. Sauté until onion is soft.

Add water and bouillon cubes. Stir to dissolve cubes.

Add remaining ingredients. Stir. Heat to boiling temperature. Garnish with chopped chives, parsley or croutons. Makes a scant 6 cups (1.25 mL).

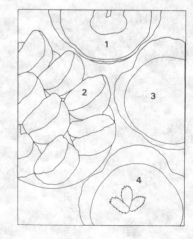

1. Blueberry Soup page 51
2. Biscuit Lips page 9
3. Cantaloupe Soup page 47
4. Strawberry Soup page 46

QUICK TOMATO CHEESE SOUP

This is it — the quickest and best gourmet soup going!

Condensed tomato soup	10 oz.	284 mL
Milk	1 1/4 cups	284 mL
Grated medium Cheddar cheese	1 cup	250 mL
Crushed basil	1/4 tsp.	1 mL

Combine all together in saucepan. Heat, stirring occasionally to melt cheese and blend flavors. Makes about 2½ cups (560 mL).

RUSH ASPARAGUS SOUP

A smooth soup, quick as a wink to prepare. May be served hot or cold. Easy to double.

Canned asparagus cuts with tips (including juice)	12 oz.	341 mL
Condensed cream of mushroom soup	10 oz.	284 mL
Dried onion flakes	1 tbsp.	15 mL
Milk	1 cup	250 mL
Pepper sprinkle		
Chives or sour cream for garnish		

Put asparagus with juice into blender. Add mushroom soup and onion. Blend until smooth. Pour into saucepan.

Stir in milk. Sprinkle with a little pepper. Bring to a gentle boil. Cover and simmer 5 minutes. Serve hot or chill to serve cold. Garnish with chopped chives or a dollop of sour cream on each serving. Makes 3 generous cups (750 mL).

CHICKEN TOMATO SOUP

Made from the shelf. Especially good.

Condensed cream of chicken soup	10 oz.	284 mL
Condensed cream of mushroom soup	10 oz.	284 mL
Water	2½ cups	568 mL
Canned tomatoes - or 2 lbs. (1 kg) fresh tomatoes, peeled and chopped	14 oz.	398 mL
Finely chopped onion	½ cup	125 mL
Dry white wine (optional)	2 tsp.	10 mL
Salt	½ tsp.	2 mL
Pepper	¼ tsp.	1 mL
Thyme (optional)	⅛ tsp.	0.5 mL
Sugar	1 tsp.	5 mL
Parsley flakes	1 tsp.	5 mL
Parsley or croutons for garnish		

Measure all ingredients into large saucepan. Bring to boil. Simmer, covered, about 15 minutes. Garnish with fresh chopped parsley or croutons. Makes about 5 cups (1.1 L).

Variation: Add chopped cooked chicken, about 1 cup (250 mL) or 6½ oz. (184 g) canned flaked chicken.

SHRIMP SOUP

Get a good fresh flavor in a hurry. Indulge.

Condensed cream of mushroom soup	10 oz.	284 mL
Milk	1¼ cups	284 mL
Green onions, sliced	2	2
Celery flakes	½ tsp.	2 mL
Garlic powder	¹⁄₁₆ tsp.	0.5 mL
Lemon juice	½ tsp.	2 mL
Shrimp, fresh or frozen	1¼ cups	300 mL

Heat all together in saucepan. Simmer about 5 minutes to cook shrimp. Makes about 3 cups (675 mL).

QUICK POTATO SOUP

Good, fast and wholesome. A meat and potato soup.

Condensed cream of potato soup	20 oz.	568 mL
Milk (using half cream is best)	2½ cups	568 mL
Canned flaked ham	6½ oz.	184 g
Cheese slices, broken up	4	4

Put all ingredients into large saucepan. Heat over medium heat, stirring often. Makes about 5 cups (1.1 L).

QUICK PEANUT SOUP

Fast and simple with a mild peanut butter flavor.

Butter or margarine	2 tbsp.	30 mL
Finely chopped onion	⅓ cup	75 mL
Smooth peanut butter	½ cup	125 mL
Condensed cream of chicken soup	20 oz.	568 mL
Milk	1¼ cups	284 mL
Water	1¼ cups	284 mL

Put butter and onion in large saucepan. Sauté until onion is soft and clear.

Stir in peanut butter until mixed. Add chicken soup, milk and water. Heat and serve. Makes about 5 cups (1.1 L).

Two fleas were wondering if they should walk home or take the dog.

INSTANT CLAM CHOWDER

Quick to prepare and loaded with clams.

Condensed New England clam chowder	10 oz.	284 mL
Water	¾ cup	175 mL
Canned minced clams with juice	5 oz.	142 g
Dried onion flakes	1 tsp.	5 mL
Water	¼ cup	50 mL
All-purpose flour	2 tbsp.	30 mL
Parsley and butter for garnish		

In medium saucepan, combine clam chowder, water, clams with juice and onion flakes. Heat.

Whisk water and flour together until smooth. Pour into clam mixture. Stir until it boils and thickens. Garnish with fresh chopped parsley and dab of butter on each serving. Makes about 3 cups (700 mL).

SHELF CRAB BISQUE

This splendid soup will suit any appetite. A snap to make.

Condensed green pea soup	10 oz.	284 mL
Condensed cream of celery soup	10 oz.	284 mL
Condensed cream of mushroom soup	10 oz.	284 mL
Condensed tomato soup	10 oz.	284 mL
Milk	1 cup	250 mL
Evaporated milk	14 oz.	398 mL
Onion powder	¼ tsp.	1 mL
Canned crab, cartilage removed	5 oz.	142 g

Put first 7 ingredients into large saucepan over medium heat. Stir occasionally while heating.

Add crab. Serve hot. Makes a generous 9 cups (2 L).

QUICK MINESTRONE

A grand shortcut to a well known soup.

Condensed chicken noodle soup	10 oz.	284 mL
Condensed vegetable soup	10 oz.	284 mL
Water	1¼ cups	284 mL
Canned kidney beans with juice	14 oz.	398 mL
Chopped cooked roast beef or scramble-fried ground beef	½ cup	125 mL

Put all ingredients into saucepan. Bring to boil. Simmer a few minutes to allow flavors to blend. Makes about 5 cups (1.1 L).

LEEK AND POTATO SOUP

Smooth and creamy.

Chicken stock, page 101	6 cups	1.3 L
Leeks, chopped, white part only	6	6
Chopped onion	½ cup	125 mL
Medium potatoes, peeled and diced	4	4
Salt	1 tsp.	5 mL
Pepper (white is best)	¼ tsp.	1 mL
Light cream	1 cup	250 mL
Chives or parsley for garnish		

Combine first 6 ingredients in large saucepan. Bring to boil. Cover and simmer for 30 minutes. Run through blender. Return to saucepan.

Stir in cream. Heat through. Garnish with chopped chives or chopped parsley. Makes about 8 cups (1.8 L).

CAULIFLOWER CHEESE SOUP

An all round favorite. The best.

Medium head of cauliflower	1	1
Chicken stock, page 101	2 cups	500 mL
Butter or margarine	¼ cup	50 mL
Chopped onion	¼ cup	50 mL
All-purpose flour	¼ cup	60 mL
Salt	½ tsp.	2 mL
Pepper	⅛ tsp.	0.5 mL
Milk	2 cups	500 mL
Grated medium Cheddar cheese	1 cup	250 mL
Buttered bread crumbs for garnish		
Parsley		

Cook cauliflower in chicken stock until tender. Do not drain. Cool a bit. Run through blender to desired texture. Set aside.

Melt butter in saucepan. Add onion and sauté until limp. Do not brown.

Mix in flour, salt and pepper. Add milk. Heat and stir until it boils and thickens.

Add cheese and cauliflower mixture. Stir to heat and melt cheese. Garnish with buttered bread crumbs. Parsley may be added as an ingredient or as a garnish. Makes about 5 cups (1.25 L).

CREAM OF CAULIFLOWER SOUP: Omit cheese. Excellent.

CAULIFLOWER SOUP: Use water instead of milk.

A hula dance is only a shake in the grass.

CREAM OF CUCUMBER SOUP

A creamy-white soup that can be frozen. Delicious served hot and with a slight variation can be served chilled.

Butter or margarine	3 tbsp.	50 mL
Peeled, seeded and chopped cucumber	3 cups	700 mL
Medium onion, finely chopped	1	1
All-purpose flour	2 tbsp.	30 mL
Salt	1 tsp.	5 mL
Pepper (white is best)	1/8 tsp.	0.5 mL
Lemon juice	1 tbsp.	15 mL
Milk	2 cups	450 mL
Dry dill weed	1/4 tsp.	1 mL
Sour cream (optional)	1/4 cup	50 mL
Fresh dill weed for garnish		

Melt butter in frying pan. For easy removal of seeds, cut peeled cucumbers in half lengthwise, then use spoon as a scoop. Add cucumber and onion to butter. Sauté until about half of the cucumber liquid has evaporated, about 10 minutes.

Mix in flour, salt and pepper. Stir in lemon juice, milk and dill weed. Heat and stir until it boils and thickens. Cool slightly. Run through blender. If you prefer chunky soup, omit blender step. May be frozen at this point.

To serve, heat to simmering temperature. Whisk in sour cream, (also good without), and serve. Fresh dill weed makes a good garnish. Makes about 3 cups (700 mL).

CHILLED CUCUMBER SOUP: Use chicken broth instead of milk.

Paré Pointer

If you keep overeating you will get thick at your stomach.

CORN SOUP

This wonderful soup has been a family favorite forever.

Milk	**3¹/₂ cups**	**800 mL**
Finely chopped onion (optional)	**2 tbsp.**	**30 mL**
Butter or margarine	**1 tsp.**	**5 mL**
Canned cream style corn	**28 oz.**	**796 mL**
Milk	**¹/₂ cup**	**125 mL**
All-purpose flour	**2 tbsp.**	**30 mL**
Salt	**1 tsp.**	**5 mL**
Pepper	**¹/₈ tsp.**	**0.5 mL**
Butter, chives or parsley for garnish		

Heat first amount of milk in large heavy saucepan.

Sauté onion in butter until clear and soft. Put into cone-shaped ricer.

Add corn to onion. Press through cone ricer. If you don't have a cone-shaped ricer, onion and corn may be puréed in blender. Rub through strainer if it isn't smooth enough.

Mix second amount of milk with flour, salt and pepper until no lumps remain. Stir into hot milk until it boils and thickens. Add corn and onion mixture. Heat through. Serve with a dab of butter, chopped chives or parsley. Makes about 7¹/₂ cups (1.7 L).

Pictured on page 71.

Alcohol preserves a lot of things, but not dignity.

There are so many ways to stretch this soup, you will have a hard time deciding which to try first. Great if unexpected guests turn up at the last minute.

Canned mixed vegetables, drained, reserve juice	**14 oz.**	**398 mL**
Butter or margarine	**2 tbsp.**	**30 mL**
Chopped onion	**⅓ cup**	**75 mL**
Chopped celery	**1 tbsp.**	**15 mL**
All-purpose flour	**2 tbsp.**	**30 mL**
Dry mustard powder	**1 tsp.**	**5 mL**
Salt	**¾ tsp.**	**3 mL**
Pepper	**⅛ tsp.**	**0.5 mL**
Chicken bouillon powder	**4 tsp.**	**20 mL**
Reserved juice plus water to make	**2 cups**	**500 mL**
Milk	**2 cups**	**400 mL**
Soft processed cheese, cut up (Velveeta is good)	**4 oz.**	**125 g**

Set vegetables and juice aside.

Melt butter in large saucepan. Add onion and celery. Sauté until clear and soft.

Mix in flour, mustard powder, salt, pepper and chicken bouillon powder. Add juice, water and milk. Stir until it boils and thickens slightly.

Add vegetables and cheese. Stir to melt. Makes about 6 cups (1.35 L).

TOMATO CHEESE SOUP: Add 14 oz. (398 mL) canned tomatoes, mashed. Heat through. Gives a different flavor and adds 1½ cups (350 mL) to quantity.

TUNA CHEESE SOUP: Add 6½ oz. (184 g) canned tuna, drained, to soup. Break apart with spoon.

MACARONI CHEESE SOUP: Cook ½ cup (125 mL) cut macaroni according to package directions. Drain. Add to soup.

CREAM OF CHICKEN SOUP

Nice creamy texture to this agreeable dish. Freezes well.

Butter or margarine	1/3 cup	75 mL
All-purpose flour	1/3 cup	75 mL
Milk	1/2 cup	125 mL
Cereal cream or half and half	1/2 cup	125 mL
Chicken stock, page 101	3 cups	750 mL
Cooked chicken, cut in strips or cubes	1 cup	250 mL
Paprika, parsley or chives for garnish		

Melt butter in saucepan. Mix in flour. Add milk, cream and chicken stock. Stir and heat until it boils and thickens.

Add chicken and heat to boiling temperature. Garnish with a sprinkle of paprika in center or use chopped parsley or chopped chives. Makes about 4 cups (1 L).

Pictured on page 89.

CREAM OF CELERY SOUP

One of the easiest to make from scratch.

Milk	2 cups	500 mL
Finely diced celery	1 1/2 cups	375 mL
Chopped onion	1/4 cup	50 mL
Butter or margarine	2 tbsp.	30 mL
All-purpose flour	3 tbsp.	60 mL
Salt	1 tsp.	5 mL
Pepper (white is best)	1/4 tsp.	1 mL
Milk	3 cups	750 mL

In heavy saucepan, put first amount of milk, celery, onion and butter. Bring to a boil. Cover and simmer until onion is tender.

Mix flour, salt and pepper with about 1/4 of the second amount of milk until no lumps remain. Stir into simmering soup until it boils and thickens. Stir in remaining milk. Makes about 5 cups (1.25 L).

Made with lots of mushrooms.

Butter or margarine	¼ cup	50 mL
Chopped onion	½ cup	125 mL
Fresh mushrooms, sliced or chopped	1 lb.	500 g
All-purpose flour	¼ cup	60 mL
Salt	½ tsp.	2 mL
Pepper	¼ tsp.	1 mL
Garlic powder - or 1 clove, minced	¼ tsp.	1 mL
Beef stock, page 102	1 cup	250 mL
Chicken stock, page 101	1 cup	250 mL
Milk	1 cup	250 mL
Cream, light or heavy	1 cup	250 mL
White wine (optional but good)	4 tsp.	25 mL

Put butter, onion and mushrooms in large pot. Sauté until onion is soft and clear.

Add flour, salt, pepper and garlic powder. Mix in. Stir in beef and chicken stock and milk. Heat and stir until it boils and thickens.

Stir in cream and wine. Bring to boiling temperature and serve. Makes about 5 cups (1.1 L).

A farmer minds his peas. An actor minds his cues.

PEPPER POT SOUP

This extraordinary soup will quickly become a favorite. A large recipe, it freezes well. Excellent.

Water	4 cups	1 L
Chicken bouillon powder	4 tbsp.	60 mL
Good size potatoes, shredded	2	2
Medium carrots, shredded	2	2
Celery stalks, chopped	2	2
Medium onions, chopped	2	2
Green pepper, finely chopped	1	1
All-purpose flour	1/2 cup	125 mL
Salt	2 tsp.	10 mL
Pepper	1/2 tsp.	2 mL
Water	1 cup	250 mL
Milk	6 cups	1.5 L

Mix first 7 ingredients together in large saucepan. Bring to boil. Cover and simmer about 20 minutes.

Mix flour, salt, pepper and water together in small container until no lumps remain. Stir into simmering soup to thicken slightly.

Add milk. Heat through. Check for seasoning. Makes about 12½ cups (2.8 L).

Pictured on page 53.

CREAM OF CARROT SOUP

An excellent flavor. Blend to whatever texture you like.

Peeled and cut up carrot	4 cups	1 L
Chicken stock, page 101	2 cups	500 mL
Chopped onion	1 cup	250 mL
Butter or margarine	3 tbsp.	50 mL
All-purpose flour	3 tbsp.	50 mL
Salt	1 tsp.	5 mL
Pepper	1/8 tsp.	0.5 mL
Seasoned salt	1/4 tsp.	1 mL
Milk	4 cups	1 L

(continued on next page)

Combine carrot, stock and onion in saucepan. Cook until vegetables are tender. Do not drain. Cool a bit. Run through blender. Set aside.

Melt butter in saucepan over medium heat. Stir in flour, salt and pepper. Add milk. Heat and stir until it boils and thickens. Add carrot mixture. Reheat and serve. Makes 7 cups (1.75 L).

CARROT CHOWDER: Cook 1⅓ cups (300 mL) diced potato along with the carrot and onion. Has a similar flavor but a touch more mellow.

CURRIED CARROT SOUP: Add ½ tsp. (2 mL) curry powder with flour. Quite mild in flavor.

SPUD SPECIAL

This chunky potato soup has carrots added for color. A satisfying soup. Large vegetable pieces don't freeze well.

Butter or margarine	3 tbsp.	50 mL
Large onion, sliced	1	1
Thinly sliced carrot	½ cup	125 mL
Diced celery	½ cup	125 mL
Garlic clove, minced	1	1
Diced potato	4 cups	1 L
Chicken stock, page 101	2 cups	500 mL
Salt	1½ tsp.	7 mL
Pepper	¼ tsp.	1 mL
Parsley flakes	1 tsp.	5 mL
Milk	2 cups	500 mL
Grated Cheddar cheese for garnish	½ cup	125 mL

Put first 5 ingredients into large saucepan. Sauté vegetables until onion is soft and clear.

Add potato, chicken stock, salt, pepper and parsley. Bring to a boil. Cover and simmer slowly until vegetables are cooked. Stir occasion-ally.

Stir in milk. Heat without boiling.

Garnish with grated cheese. Makes generous 5 cups (1.25 L).

Pictured on page 107.

PUMPKIN SOUP

Creamy and different. A favorite of witches.

Butter or margarine	2 tbsp.	30 mL
Chopped onion	½ cup	125 mL
Chicken stock, page 101	2 cups	500 mL
Good size potato	1	1
Salt	½ tsp.	2 mL
Pepper	¼ tsp.	1 mL
Thyme	⅛ tsp.	0.5 mL
Canned pumpkin - or use fresh, cooked and mashed	14 oz.	398 mL
Milk	2 cups	500 mL

Put butter and onion into large saucepan. Sauté until clear and soft. Do not brown.

Add chicken stock, potato, salt, pepper and thyme. Bring to boil. Simmer gently to cook potato. Cool a bit. Run through blender. Return to saucepan.

Stir in pumpkin and milk. Heat through. Thin with additional milk if needed. Add more salt and pepper if necessary. Makes about 6 cups (1.3 L).

LETTUCE SOUP

A terrific way to use garden lettuce even if it is the leaf variety. Add more to make thicker soup if you like.

Butter or margarine	2 tbsp.	30 mL
Finely chopped onion	2 tbsp.	30 mL
All-purpose flour	2 tbsp.	30 mL
Salt	½ tsp.	2 mL
Pepper	⅛ tsp.	0.5 mL
Chicken stock, page 101	3 cups	750 mL
Shredded head lettuce, firmly packed	4 cups	1 L
Rich creamy milk	1 cup	250 mL

(continued on next page)

Melt butter in large saucepan. Add onion and sauté until soft and clear.

Mix in flour, salt and pepper. Stir in chicken stock until it boils and thickens slightly.

Add lettuce. Simmer for about 3 minutes.

Add creamy milk. Heat through. Makes about 4½ cups (1 L).

Pictured on page 125.

CREAMED VEGETABLE SOUP

Vegetables in a light and creamy broth. Eye appealing.

Celery stalks, thinly sliced	2	2
Medium carrots, thinly sliced	2	2
Large onion, sliced or diced	1	1
Good size potato, cubed	1	1
Diced turnip	1 cup	250 mL
Cut green beans (optional)	½ cup	125 mL
Water	4 cups	1 L
Salt	1 tsp.	5 mL
Pepper	¼ tsp.	1 mL
Peas, fresh or frozen	½ cup	125 mL
All-purpose flour	¼ cup	60 mL
Milk	1 cup	250 mL

Put first 9 ingredients into large pot. Bring to boil. Cover and simmer about 20 minutes.

Add peas. Simmer 5 minutes more.

Mix flour with milk until no lumps remain. Stir into simmering soup until it boils and thickens. Test for salt. You may need to add ½ tsp. (2 mL) more. Makes about 7 cups (1.5 L).

Pictured on page 71.

VEGETABLE SOUP: Omit flour and milk. Add 1 cup (250 mL) tomato juice. Dandy flavor.

PURÉE OF VEGETABLE SOUP

This purée of vegetables can be made from frozen mixed vegetables, clean-the-fridge vegetables or your own favorites. The addition of spinach makes it a darker green which may be preferable.

Butter or margarine	**2 tbsp.**	**30 mL**
Chopped onion	**½ cup**	**125 mL**
All-purpose flour	**1 tbsp.**	**15 mL**
Salt	**½ tsp.**	**2 mL**
Pepper	**¼ tsp.**	**1 mL**
Celery salt	**⅛ tsp.**	**0.5 mL**
Chicken stock, page 101	**2 cups**	**500 mL**
Cooked vegetables, puréed	**2½ cups**	**625 mL**
Light cream or milk	**1 cup**	**250 mL**
Chives or green onions for garnish		

Melt butter in large saucepan. Add onion. Sauté until clear and soft.

Mix in flour, salt, pepper and celery salt. Add chicken stock and vegetables. Purée in blender. Return to saucepan. Stir until it boils and thickens a bit.

Add cream. Heat through. Garnish with chopped chives or chopped green onions. Makes about 5⅓ cups (1.2 L).

Note: If you have no leftover vegetables, try a combination of carrot, turnip, potato, and green beans.

1. Ribbon Sandwiches page 113
2. Elegant Consommé page 45

CREAM OF TOMATO SOUP

Use home-canned tomatoes or commercial. Exceptionally flavorful. Doesn't freeze well.

Canned tomatoes	4 cups	1 L
Medium onion, chopped	1	1
Whole cloves	4	4
Small bay leaf	1	1
Salt	1 tsp.	5 mL
Pepper	1/4 tsp.	1 mL
Granulated sugar	1 tbsp.	15 mL
Baking soda	1/4 tsp.	2 mL
Milk	2 cups	500 mL
All-purpose flour	2 tbsp.	30 mL
Water	1/4 cup	50 mL
Cream, cheese or chives for garnish		

Put first 7 ingredients into large saucepan. Bring to boil. Cover and simmer for about 20 minutes. Put through cone ricer or food mill. A blender can be used, then put through sieve to remove seeds. Return to pot.

Stir in baking soda to keep from curdling.

Heat milk in separate large saucepan. Mix flour with water until no lumps remain. Stir into simmering milk until it boils and thickens a bit. Pour hot tomato mixture into thickened milk. Do not boil or it will curdle. Garnish with cream swirl, grated cheese or chopped chives. Makes about 6 cups (1.3 L).

Paré Pointer

A baby duck walks softly because it can't walk, hardly.

CREAM OF SPINACH SOUP

Serve as a creamy soup with green chopped spinach or run through blender until it has a speckled appearance.

Butter or margarine	¼ cup	50 mL
Chopped onion	2 cups	500 mL
All-purpose flour	6 tbsp.	100 mL
Salt	1 tsp.	5 mL
Pepper	¼ tsp.	1 mL
Chicken stock, page 101	6 cups	1.5 L
Frozen chopped spinach, thawed and squeezed dry	10 oz.	300 g
Light cream	1 cup	250 mL

Put butter and onion into large saucepan. Sauté until clear and soft.

Mix in flour, salt and pepper. Stir in chicken stock until it boils and thickens.

Add spinach. Simmer 5 minutes to cook.

Stir in cream. Heat without boiling and serve. Makes approximately 9 cups (2 L).

Note: To use fresh spinach, chop and measure 6 cups (1.35 L), packed down firmly. Approximately 2 bunches needed.

TOMATO SOUP

Tomatoes and milk are heated separately, then combined to produce this old fashioned soup. Doesn't freeze well.

Canned tomatoes	14 oz.	398 mL
Milk	2 cups	450 mL
All-purpose flour	1 tbsp.	15 mL
Salt	½ tsp.	2 mL
Pepper	⅛ tsp.	0.5 mL
Granulated sugar	½ tsp.	2 mL
Milk	¼ cup	50 mL
Baking soda	¼ tsp.	1 mL

(continued on next page)

Heat tomatoes in small saucepan. Break up into small pieces.

Heat first amount of milk in another saucepan.

Mix flour, salt, pepper, sugar and second amount of milk together in small dish until no lumps remain. Stir into simmering milk until it boils and thickens.

Stir baking soda into hot tomatoes. Stir hot tomatoes slowly into hot milk. Makes a generous 3 cups (750 mL).

SMOOTH TOMATO SOUP: Smooth tomatoes in blender before heating.

BROCCOLI CHEESE SOUP

An absolutely yummy soup. Delectable.

Chopped onion	¼ cup	60 mL
Butter or margarine	1 tbsp.	15 mL
Milk	2½ cups	600 mL
Chicken bouillon powder	1 tbsp.	15 mL
Frozen broccoli, chopped - save a bit for garnish	10 oz.	284 g
Salt	½ tsp.	2 mL
Pepper	⅛ tsp.	0.5 mL
Grated medium Cheddar cheese	1 cup	250 mL

Put onion and butter in saucepan. Sauté until clear and soft.

Add next 5 ingredients. Bring to boil. Cover and simmer until vegeta–bles are cooked. Cool a bit then chop to desired coarseness in batches in blender. Return to saucepan.

Add cheese. Stir to melt. Garnish with a piece of broccoli. Makes about 3⅓ cups (750 mL).

CREAM OF BROCCOLI SOUP: Omit cheese. Mix 1 tbsp. (15 mL) all-purpose flour into sautéed onions before adding milk.

BROCCOLI SOUP. Omit cheese. Use water instead of milk. Double chicken bouillon. Add 1 slice bacon, crispy-fried and crumbled. Mix 1 tbsp. (15 mL) all-purpose flour into sautéed onions before adding milk.

CREAM OF GREEN BEAN SOUP

Meaty, flavorful, appetizing.

Butter or margarine	½ cup	125 mL
Green string beans, fresh or frozen, cut in short pieces	6 cups	1.5 L
Finely chopped onion	¼ cup	50 mL
All-purpose flour	¼ cup	50 mL
Salt	2 tsp.	10 mL
Pepper	¼ tsp.	1 mL
Milk	3½ cups	800 mL
Water	3 cups	700 mL
Chicken stock, page 101	1 cup	250 mL
Canned corned beef, diced	12 oz.	341 mL
Sour cream or Cheddar cheese for garnish		

Melt butter in large saucepan. Add beans and onion. Sauté until onion is clear.

Stir in flour, salt and pepper. Add milk, water and chicken broth. Stir and cook until thickened.

Crumble corned beef into bean-milk mixture. Simmer until beans are cooked. Serve with dollop of sour cream or grated Cheddar cheese. Makes about 10 cups (2.25 L).

Pictured on page 71.

She thought a jitterbug was a nervous insect.

A grand flavor to enjoy during any season. Do not freeze.

Butter or margarine	2 tbsp.	30 mL
Chopped onion	¼ cup	50 mL
All-purpose flour	2 tbsp.	30 mL
Salt	½ tsp.	2 mL
Pepper	¼ tsp.	1 mL
Milk	2 cups	450 mL
Chicken stock, page 101	1 cup	250 mL
Frozen asparagus - or 2 cups (500 mL) fresh	10 oz.	300 g
Cheddar or Parmesan cheese for garnish		

Put butter and onion in saucepan. Sauté until clear and soft.

Mix in flour, salt and pepper. Add milk and chicken stock. Cook and stir until it boils and thickens.

Cook asparagus in very little water. Drain and chop. Add to the sauce. Run through blender if a smooth texture is desired. May need more salt. Serve hot, garnished with grated Cheddar or Parmesan cheese. Makes about 3½ cups (750 mL).

You know what happens to naughty pigs? They become devilled ham.

CREAMY PEANUT SOUP

This creamy soup will surprise and delight young and old alike.

Butter or margarine	3 tbsp.	50 mL
Small onion, chopped finely	1	1
Celery stalks, diced	2	2
Shredded carrot	½ cup	125 mL
All-purpose flour	2 tbsp.	30 mL
Chicken stock, page 101	2 cups	500 mL
Smooth peanut butter	1 cup	250 mL
Light cream or milk	2½ cups	600 mL
Lemon juice	2 tsp.	10 mL
Salt	¼ tsp.	1 mL
Ground peanuts for garnish		

Put butter, onion, celery and carrot in saucepan. Sauté until onion is clear and soft. Do not brown.

Stir in flour. Add chicken stock. Heat and stir until it boils and thickens and vegetables are cooked.

Add peanut butter. Stir to mix. Add cream or milk, lemon juice and salt. Heat and serve. Garnish with ground peanuts. Makes about 5 cups (1.1 L).

PEANUT SOUP: Use only ½ cup (125 mL) peanut butter for a milder flavor.

ARTICHOKE SOUP

Thick and creamy with a good, sharp flavor.

Canned artichoke hearts, drained	28 oz.	796 mL
Egg	1	1
Condensed chicken broth	20 oz.	568 mL
Butter or margarine	3 tbsp.	50 mL
All-purpose flour	3 tbsp.	50 mL
Salt	⅛ tsp.	0.5 mL
Pepper (white is best)	⅛ tsp.	0.5 mL
Light cream (cereal cream or half and half)	1 cup	250 mL
Sour cream or chives for garnish		

(continued on next page)

Put artichoke hearts into blender. Add egg and some chicken broth. Blend until smooth. Set aside.

Melt butter in saucepan over medium heat. Mix in flour, salt and pepper. Add cream, stirring until it boils and thickens. Gradually stir in contents of blender and remaining chicken broth. Heat. Taste for seasoning, adding more salt and pepper if needed. Serve hot. A dab of sour cream or a sprinkle of chopped chives in the center makes a good garnish. Makes about 6 cups (1.3 L).

VICHYSSOISE

Vichyssoise (VISH–ee–swahz) is still a classic. It is rich with cream and served cold.

Butter or margarine	3 tbsp.	50 mL
Leeks, white part only, sliced	2	2
Medium onion, chopped	1	1
Medium potatoes, sliced	5	5
Chicken stock, page 101	4 cups	1 L
Salt	1 tsp.	5 mL
Pepper (white is best)	1/4 tsp.	1 mL
Light cream or milk	1 1/2 cups	350 mL
Heavy cream	1 cup	250 mL
Chives for garnish		

Put butter, leek and onion into large saucepan. Sauté until onion is clear and very soft. Do not brown.

Add potato, chicken stock, salt and pepper. Bring to boil. Cover and simmer until potato is cooked, about 20 minutes. Purée in blender. Return to saucepan.

Add light cream. If soup seems grainy rather than smooth, put through sieve. Stir in heavy cream. Chill. To serve, sprinkle with chopped chives. Makes about 8 1/2 cups (2 L).

ALMOND SOUP

Begin your special dinner party with this creamy, delicately flavored soup.

Butter or margarine	3 tbsp.	50 mL
All-purpose flour	2 tbsp.	30 mL
Salt	1/2 tsp.	2 mL
Pepper (white is best)	1/8 tsp.	0.5 mL
Chicken stock, page 101	2 cups	500 mL
Light cream	1 cup	250 mL
Ground almonds	1 cup	250 mL
White wine to taste (optional)		

Melt butter in medium saucepan. Stir in flour, salt and pepper. Add chicken stock, stirring, until it boils and thickens.

Stir in cream, almonds and wine, if using. Heat and serve. Makes about 3¼ cups (750 mL).

TOMATO CONSOMMÉ

Although you could never guess, this appetizer soup gets its special taste from soy sauce. Dark and clear.

Beef bouillon cube - 1/5 oz. (6 g) size	1	1
Boiling water	1 cup	250 mL
Tomato juice	2 cups	500 mL
Lemon juice	1 tsp.	5 mL
Soy sauce	1 tsp.	5 mL
Granulated sugar	1/2 tsp.	2 mL
Chives for garnish		

Dissolve bouillon cube in boiling water in saucepan.

Add tomato juice, lemon juice, soy sauce and sugar. Bring to boiling temperature. Garnish with chopped chives and serve. Makes about 3 cups (675 mL).

ELEGANT CONSOMMÉ

Sparkling clear broth with slivers of vegetables in the bottom. Tasty but not filling. A perfect appetizer.

Carrot slivers	1 tbsp.	15 mL
Celery slivers	1 tbsp.	15 mL
Turnip slivers	1 tbsp.	15 mL
Chopped green onion	1 tbsp.	15 mL
Condensed chicken broth	10 oz.	284 mL
Water	1¼ cups	284 mL
Chives for garnish		

Put all ingredients into saucepan. Bring to boil. Cover and simmer until vegetables are tender. Garnish with a few chopped chives if desired. Makes about 2⅔ cups (600 mL).

Pictured on page 35.

FRUIT SOUP

Scandinavian in origin, this soup is a glistening, dried fruit treat. Ingredients are easy to keep on hand. Good as pre-dinner soup or as dessert.

Water	4 cups	1 L
Canned pineapple juice	19 oz.	540 mL
Packaged mixed dried fruit (prunes, apricots, apples, peaches) cut in pieces. Push down gently to measure	2 cups	450 mL
Raisins or currants	½ cup	125 mL
Prepared orange juice	½ cup	125 mL
Cinnamon	¼ tsp.	1 mL
Granulated sugar	⅓ cup	75 mL
Minute tapioca	2 tbsp.	30 mL

Put water and pineapple juice into large saucepan. Add remaining ingredients. Bring to a boil over medium heat. Cover. Simmer gently for 30 minutes. Cool. Serve chilled. Makes 4 cups (900 mL).

APRICOT SOUP

Tangy and refreshing. Nice color and fairly thick.

Canned apricots with juice	28 oz.	796 mL
Light cream or milk	1 cup	250 mL
Lemon juice	1 tbsp.	15 mL
Fresh mint leaves for garnish		

Run apricots and juice through blender. Mix with cream and lemon juice. Serve chilled. Garnish with fresh mint leaves. Makes about 4 cups (900 mL).

FRESH APRICOT SOUP: Cook 2 cups (500 mL) apricot halves with 1 cup (250 mL) granulated sugar and 1 cup (250 mL) water, until tender. Run all through blender until smooth. Add cream and lemon juice as above. Makes about 4 cups (900 mL).

STRAWBERRY SOUP

Served before or after a meal, this cold soup is a winner every time.

Sliced fresh strawberries	2 cups	500 mL
Prepared orange juice	½ cup	125 mL
Water	½ cup	125 mL
Granulated sugar	½ cup	125 mL
Cornstarch	1 tbsp.	15 mL
Water	1 tbsp.	15 mL
Sherry (optional)	2 tsp.	10 mL
Sour cream and strawberry leaf for garnish		

Put strawberries, orange juice, first amount of water and sugar into saucepan. Bring to a boil. Simmer until cooked.

Mix cornstarch with second amount of water. Stir into simmering strawberries to thicken. Chill.

Add sherry. Serve cold with a dollop of sour cream. Garnish with strawberry leaf. Makes 2½ cups (650 mL).

Pictured on page 17.

(continued on next page)

RASPBERRY SOUP: Use raspberries instead of strawberries.

STRAWBERRY RHUBARB SOUP: Cook 1 cup (250 mL) rhubarb with strawberry mixture. Do not thicken with cornstarch. Purée in blender. Rub through sieve to remove rhubarb strings. Chill to serve. No need to add more sugar. Just the right tartness.

CANTALOUPE SOUP

Resembles a cool refreshing milkshake. Gorgeous color. May also be served hot.

Ripe cantaloupe, cut up	**3**	**3**
Prepared orange juice	**2 cups**	**500 mL**
Granulated sugar	**1/4 cup**	**50 mL**
Lime juice (or lemon)	**1 tsp.**	**5 mL**
White wine	**1/4 cup**	**50 mL**
Cream for garnish		

Smooth all ingredients in blender, in batches. Taste for sweetness, adding a bit more sugar if needed. Serve chilled. A swirl of cream makes an attractive garnish. Makes about 3½ cups (800 mL).

Pictured on page 17.

Mother ghost to child ''Don't spook until you're spooken to.''

CHERRY SOUP

A pleasant tang. Easy to double or triple the recipe. Most attractive served with a sour or whipped cream garnish.

Canned Bing cherries	14 oz.	398 mL
Red wine vinegar	1 tbsp.	15 mL
Granulated sugar	2 tsp.	10 mL
Cinnamon	1/8 tsp.	0.5 mL
Salt sprinkle (optional)		

Sour cream, whipped cream or heavy
cream for garnish

Drain juice from cherries into blender. Pit the cherries and add to blender. Add wine vinegar, sugar, cinnamon and a light sprinkle of salt. Blend until smooth. Chill.

Serve with a dab of sour cream or plain whipped cream, or pour a bit of heavy cream in center of bowl. Swirl with spoon. Makes about 1¾ cups (400 mL).

SOUR CHERRY SOUP: Canned sour cherries may be used instead of sweet. Add granulated sugar to taste.

A stolen sweet could be hot chocolate.

AVOCADO SOUP

First choice — thick and so smooth. Do not freeze.

Very ripe avocados, medium size	3	3
Chopped onion	1/4 cup	50 mL
Light cream (cereal cream or half and half)	1 cup	250 mL
Condensed cream of chicken soup	10 oz.	284 mL
Seasoned salt	1/2 tsp.	2 mL
Chives for garnish		

Peel avocados and cut into chunks. Put into blender along with onion, cream, chicken soup and seasoned salt. Purée. Serve chilled with a few chopped chives sprinkled in center. Makes about 3 cups (700 mL).

BUTTERMILK SOUP

You would never guess this contains buttermilk. White and smooth as satin. Superb.

Egg yolks	3	3
Granulated sugar	1/2 cup	125 mL
Lemon juice	1 tsp.	5 mL
Grated lemon rind	1/2 tsp.	2 mL
Vanilla	1 tsp.	5 mL
Buttermilk	4 cups	1 L
Whipped cream for garnish	1 cup	250 mL
Strawberry jam for garnish	2 tbsp.	30 mL

Beat egg yolks in mixing bowl. Add sugar, lemon juice, rind and vanilla. Beat well.

Slowly beat in buttermilk. Chill until ready to serve.

To serve, put a dollop of whipped cream in center of each bowl. Top cream with a bit of strawberry jam. Makes about 4 1/2 cups (1 L).

APPLE BROTH SOUP

An unusual combination of apple, onion and chicken stock. Very tasty with a hint of apple flavor. A hot soup.

Butter or margarine	3 tbsp.	50 mL
Chopped onion	1 cup	250 mL
Apples, peeled, cored and sliced	3	3
Cinnamon	1/4 tsp.	1 mL
Chicken stock, page 101	4 cups	900 mL
Cinnamon sticks (optional)		

Put butter and onion into pot. Sauté until onion is soft and clear.

Add apple and cinnamon. Sauté until apple softens. Run through blender to smooth.

Heat chicken stock and apple mixture together until piping hot. Serve. A cinnamon stick in each bowl is very appropriate. Makes a generous 7 cups (1.5 L).

Variation: Add 1/4 tsp. (1 mL) curry powder. Good.

APPLE SOUP

Similar to cheery apple cider. A clear golden broth over tiny apple chunks.

Apple juice	4 cups	1 L
Apples, peeled, cored and diced	4	4
Cinnamon	1/2 tsp.	2 mL
Lemon juice	1 tsp.	5 mL
Brown sugar, packed	1/2 cup	125 mL
Cinnamon sticks (optional)		

Simmer all together, covered, in large pot until apples are barely tender. Chill. This looks especially attractive served with a cinnamon stick in each bowl. Serve cold. Makes about 5½ cups (1.25 L).

Although this may be served cold, it is delicious hot. The sour cream garnish is also good when stirred into the soup.

Water	**2 cups**	**500 mL**
Blueberries, fresh or frozen	**2 cups**	**500 mL**
Granulated sugar	**¼ cup**	**50 mL**
Cornstarch	**1 tbsp.**	**15 mL**
Cinnamon	**¼ tsp.**	**1 mL**
Lemon juice	**1 tsp.**	**5 mL**

Sour cream (or yogurt) for garnish
Cinnamon sticks (optional)

Simmer first six ingredients together until blueberries are cooked. Run through blender.

Serve hot with a dollop of sour cream. A cinnamon stick may be added to each bowl for an extra touch. Makes about 3 cups (700 mL).

Pictured on page 17.

Combine a gangster and a dustman for organized grime.

COCK-A-LEEKIE SOUP

From Scotland, this was traditionally served as a broth-type soup with the meat removed for the main course.

Fowl (stewing hen)	3 lbs.	1.5 kg
Water	8 cups	1.75 L
Chicken bouillon cubes - $1/5$ oz. (6 g) size	2	2
Leeks, sliced, white part only	6	6
Barley - or long grain rice	6 tbsp.	100 mL
Dried prunes, quartered	6	6
Salt	$2^1/4$ tsp.	11 mL
Pepper	$1/4$ tsp.	1 mL

Combine fowl, water and bouillon cubes in large pot. Cover and simmer 45 to 60 minutes or until chicken is cooked. Remove chicken. Take meat from bones. Cut meat into small pieces and return to pot.

Add remaining ingredients. Bring to boil. Cover and simmer for about 40 minutes or until barley is soft. Makes a generous 6 cups (1.5 L).

Note: Chicken parts may be substituted for fowl. Backs and thighs, about 2 lbs. (1 kg) should do it.

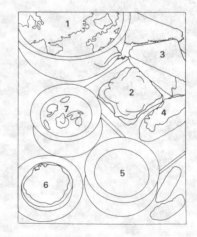

1. Old Time Borscht page 56
2. Cheese Puffs page 139
3. Beef Slaw Sandwich page 104
4. Frankly Cheese Buns page 137
5. Pepper Pot Soup page 30
6. Bologna Buns page 135
7. Tortellini Soup page 64

An Anglo-Indian dish (Mul–i–gah–TAH–nee) is sometimes known as chicken curry. British troops in India became so fond of this, that now it is as much "theirs as theirs". If the curry makes you wary, start with less.

Butter or margarine	1/4 cup	50 mL
Medium onions, chopped	2	2
Curry powder	2 tbsp.	30 mL
Medium apple, peeled and diced	1	1
All-purpose flour	1/4 cup	50 mL
Salt	1/2 tsp.	2 mL
Pepper	1/8 tsp.	0.5 mL
Chicken stock, page 101	6 cups	1.35 L
Cubed cooked chicken	2 cups	500 mL
Medium carrots, diced	2	2
Celery stalk, diced	1	1
Light cream	1/2 cup	125 mL

Put butter in saucepan. Add onion, curry powder and apple. Sauté until onion is soft.

Mix in flour, salt and pepper. Add chicken stock. Stir until it boils and thickens.

Add chicken, carrots, celery and cream. Simmer, covered, until vegetables are tender. Makes about 7 cups (1.75 L).

Variation: Add 1 cup (250 mL) cooked rice to the soup or place about 2 tbsp. (30 mL) in each bowl before filling.

Variation: There may be those who feel the authentic version contains no carrot or celery. Simply omit.

Most shopping carts can hold one child and a week's salary.

OLD TIME BORSCHT

This zestful, whole-meal soup uses sweet heavy cream to prepare for serving. Try it for a different flavor than sour cream. Even better tomorrow.

Spare ribs, cut short	1 lb.	500 g
Water to cover		
Large onions, chopped	2	2
Good sized carrots, diced	3	3
Coarsely shredded cabbage	1 cup	250 mL
Beets, peeled and cut into strips	3 cups	750 mL
Peas, fresh or frozen	1 cup	250 mL
Lima beans with juice (optional)	7 oz.	200 mL
Salt	2 tsp.	10 mL
Pepper	1/4 tsp.	1 mL
Vinegar	1 tbsp.	15 mL
Dry dill weed	1/2 tsp.	2 mL
Whipping cream	1/3 cup	75 mL
Sour cream (optional)		

Put spare ribs in pot. Cover with water. Bring to boil. Cover and simmer for about 1 hour or until meat is tender.

Add onion, carrot, cabbage and beet. Simmer until vegetables are cooked.

Add peas, beans, salt, pepper, vinegar and dill weed. Simmer for 5 minutes more.

Stir in whipping cream. Makes about 12 cups (2.75 L). Pass sour cream if desired.

Note: Pork steak, shoulder or chops cut bite size may be used. It will give a meatier soup. If you prefer meatless borscht, use chicken stock, page 101, instead of water.

Pictured on page 53.

By using canned beans, preparation time has been reduced. A full meal.

Bacon slices, cut into small pieces	4	4
Large onion, chopped	1	1
Ground beef	1½ lbs.	750 g
Boiling water	6 cups	1.5 L
Beef bouillon cubes - ⅕ oz. (6 g) size	6	6
Canned spaghetti sauce	2 cups	500 mL
Chopped cabbage	2 cups	500 mL
Celery stalk, chopped	1	1
Medium carrot, diced	1	1
Sliced zucchini	1 cup	250 mL
Salt	1 tsp.	5 mL
Pepper	¼ tsp.	1 mL
Garlic powder	¼ tsp.	1 mL
Canned kidney beans with juice	14 oz.	398 mL
Vermicelli, broken, or other small pasta	½ cup	125 mL

Put bacon, onion and ground beef into large pot. Sauté until bacon is cooked and onion is soft.

Combine water and bouillon cubes. Stir to dissolve. Add to onion mixture.

Add next 8 ingredients. Bring to boil. Cover and simmer 30 minutes.

Add beans and pasta. Boil 10 minutes more. Makes about 12 cups (2.7 L).

Paré Pointer

If you cross a bat with a palm tree, you have a blind date.

GREEK LEMON SOUP

Avgolemono (AV–guh–LEM–on–oh) consists chiefly of rice cooked in broth with a slight lemon flavor. Popular in Greece. Do not freeze.

Chicken stock, page 101	6 cups	1.5 L
Long grain rice	½ cup	125 mL
Eggs	4	4
Lemon juice	4 tsp.	25 mL
Pepper sprinkle (white is best)		
Chives or parsley for garnish		

Put chicken stock and rice into large saucepan. Bring to boil. Cover and simmer about 15 minutes to cook rice.

Beat eggs in medium bowl until frothy. Add lemon juice. Gradually stir in about ⅓ chicken-rice mixture. Add back to saucepan, stirring. Do not allow to return to simmer or it will curdle. Add a light sprinkle of pepper. Stir and taste before adding more. Garnish with chopped chives or chopped parsley. Makes about 6 cups (1.35 L).

EGG DROP SOUP

A tasty broth filled with threads of egg.

Chicken stock, page 101	6 cups	1.35 L
Granulated sugar	½ tsp.	2 mL
Soy sauce	1 tbsp.	15 mL
Water	1 tbsp.	15 mL
Cornstarch	1 tbsp.	15 mL
Eggs, beaten frothy	2	2

Heat chicken stock, sugar and soy sauce in saucepan until boiling.

Mix water with cornstarch. Stir into boiling stock.

Pour eggs slowly in a thin stream into boiling stock, whisking with a wire whisk or fork as you pour. Eggs will cook in threads. Serve hot. Makes about 5½ cups (1.25 L).

A large family size recipe. Gorgeous color. A meal in itself. Easy to halve recipe.

Water	12 cups	3 L
Chicken bouillon cubes - $\frac{1}{5}$ oz. (6 g) size	6	6
Medium potatoes, peeled and diced	2	2
Medium carrots, peeled and diced	2	2
Chopped celery	2 cups	500 mL
Medium onion, chopped	1	1
Tomato sauce	14 oz.	398 mL
Portuguese sausage (or ham sausage, garlic sausage or wieners), cut up	2 cups	500 mL
Salt	1 tsp.	5 mL
Pepper	$\frac{1}{4}$ tsp.	1 mL
Canned kidney beans with juice	14 oz.	398 mL
Elbow macaroni	1 cup	250 mL
Shredded cabbage, pressed down	4 cups	1 L

Put water and chicken cubes into large pot. Bring to a boil. Stir to dissolve cubes.

Add next eight ingredients. Bring to a gentle boil. Cover and simmer until vegetables are tender. Stir occasionally.

Add beans, macaroni and cabbage. Return to boil. Cover and simmer about 10 minutes more. Serve hot. Makes about 16 cups (3.5 L).

Don't eat daffydills. They are crazy pickles.

WONTONS

Filling may be made ahead, then make wontons when you get time. Make lots and freeze the extra.

Lean ground pork	½ lb.	**250 g**
Egg	1	**1**
Finely chopped green onion	3 tbsp.	**50 mL**
Soy sauce	1 tbsp.	**15 mL**
Salt	¼ tsp.	**1 mL**
Monosodium glutamate (optional)	¼ tsp.	**1 mL**
Wonton wrappers, thawed	1 lb.	**454 g**

In medium size bowl combine first 6 ingredients. If too soft to work with, add a few dry bread crumbs.

Place 1 tsp. (5 mL) filling in center of wonton wrapper. Moisten edges. Fold over, forming triangle. Press edges to seal. Moisten bottom corners, pull gently together to overlap, and press together. Freeze on tray with waxed paper between layers. Store in sealed container once frozen. Makes about 3 dozen.

A tailor's son is a son of a sew and sew.

A special soup requiring a special cabbage. Bok choy can be found in the produce section of larger grocery stores. This is a large recipe. It freezes well.

Medium bok choy	½ **head**	½ **head**
Green onions, sliced	2	2
Leek	1	1
Medium mushrooms, sliced	4	4
Chicken stock, page 101	**4 cups**	**900 mL**
Leftover roast pork, cut in 2 inch (5 cm)	½ **cup**	**125 mL**
slivers		
Water	**8 cups**	**2 L**
Wontons	32	32

Cut green leafy tops off bok choy and chop into small pieces. Cut white stalks into matchstick size pieces. Put greens and white slivers into large pot. Add green onion. Cut off bottom and green part of leek and discard. Cut white part in half crosswise. Sliver into matchstick size pieces and add to pot. Add mushrooms and chicken stock. Bring to boil. Cover and simmer for about 20 minutes.

Boil water in large pot. Using slotted spoon, add 10 wontons at a time. When they are cooked, they will rise to the top. Transfer to soup. Serve. Pass the soy sauce. Serves 8.

Note: Wontons left standing in soup too long tend to lose flavor. It is best to cook only as many as will be used, freezing the rest.

WONTON SOUP: Boil 12 to 15 wontons in 6 cups (1.5 L) chicken stock until they float. Add 3 green onions, sliced.

When geese collide in mid-air, they get goose bumps.

GAZPACHO

A Spanish specialty containing fresh vegetables. Served cold. May also be puréed and served cold or hot.

Canned tomatoes, cut up (or use fresh)	14 oz.	398 mL
Cucumber, peeled, seeded and chopped	1	1
Chopped onion	1/2 cup	125 mL
Red bell pepper, chopped	1	1
Canned tomato paste	1 tbsp.	15 mL
Red wine vinegar	1 tbsp.	30 mL
Salt	1/2 tsp.	2 mL
Pepper	1/4 tsp.	1 mL
Garlic powder	1/4 tsp.	1 mL
Olive oil (optional)	2 tbsp.	30 mL
Hot pepper sauce to taste		

Combine all ingredients in large bowl. Coarsely chop in blender in small batches, to reduce size of vegetables. Chill 4 hours. Test for seasoning before serving. Thin with tomato juice or water if necessary. Check again for seasoning. Makes about 3 cups (700 mL).

MEXICAN SOUP

A different soup. The green chilies add spice but not too much heat. Most enjoyable.

Butter or margarine	2 tbsp.	30 mL
Chopped onion	1 cup	250 mL
Chicken broth	2 cups	500 mL
Canned tomatoes, mashed	14 oz.	398 mL
Canned chopped green chilies with juice	4 oz.	113 g
Monterey Jack cheese	4 oz.	113 g
Parsley for garnish		

(continued on next page)

Put butter and onion into saucepan. Sauté until onion is clear and soft.

Add chicken broth, tomatoes and green chilies. Simmer to blend flavors and until onion is cooked.

Cut in cheese. Stir to melt. Garnish with sprigs of parsley. Makes about 4¾ cups (1.25 L).

SCOTCH BROTH

From Scotland; with lots of vegetables and thickened with barley. Traditionally made with lamb, beef may also be used.

Water	8 cups	2 L
Lamb stew meat, cut into small pieces	1 lb.	500 g
Pearl or pot barley	½ cup	125 mL
Diced turnip	1 cup	250 mL
Diced carrot	2 cups	500 mL
Medium onions, chopped	2	2
Leeks, white part only, sliced (optional)	2	2
Shredded cabbage, packed	2 cups	500 mL
Chopped celery	½ cup	125 mL
Salt	2 tsp.	10 mL
Pepper	½ tsp.	2 mL
Thyme	¼ tsp.	1 mL

Put water, lamb and barley into large saucepan. Bring to boil. Cover and simmer 1 hour.

Add remaining ingredients. Bring to boil again. Cover and simmer about 30 minutes. This is a thick soup. If you prefer, thin with water. Check seasoning. Makes about 12 cups (2.7 L).

TORTELLINI SOUP

A broth-type soup with pasta. Different and good.

Chicken stock, page 101	6 cups	1.5 L
Chopped onion	1 cup	250 mL
Chopped celery	1/2 cup	125 mL
Sliced carrot	1/2 cup	125 mL
Parsley flakes	1 tsp.	5 mL
Salt	1/2 tsp.	2 mL
Pepper	1/8 tsp.	0.5 mL
Rosemary	1/8 tsp.	0.5 mL
Sliced fresh mushrooms	1/4 cup	50 mL
Tortellini, frozen or use recipe following	24	24

Put first 8 ingredients into large saucepan. Bring to boil. Cover and simmer for 20 minutes.

Add mushrooms and tortellini. Return to boil. Cover and simmer for 15 minutes or until tortellini tests done. Makes about 5½ cups (1.25 L).

TORTELLINI FILLING

Finely chopped cooked chicken	1/2 cup	125 mL
Grated Parmesan cheese	1 tbsp.	15 mL
Water		

Mix together, adding just enough water to hold together. Use to fill tortellini.

TORTELLINI

All-purpose flour	1 cup	250 mL
Eggs	2	2
Salt	1/4 tsp.	1 mL

Mix together to form stiff dough. Divide in half. Roll 1/2 dough very thinly on lightly floured surface. Cut into 2 inch (5 cm) circles. Put 1/4 tsp. (1 mL) of filling on each, moisten edges with water, fold over and press to seal. Pull ends together away from curved side. Use a touch of water to seal. These freeze well. Makes 24.

Pictured on page 53.

A superb creation from southern Louisiana. It can contain leftovers of ham, turkey or chicken along with seafood. It is served over a mound of rice in a flat bowl. Don't be intimidated by the length of the recipe. If time runs out, continue later. Gumbo is better the second day anyway.

Butter or margarine	1/4 cup	50 mL
All-purpose flour	2 tbsp.	30 mL
Large onion, chopped	1	1
Hot water	2 cups	500 mL
Chopped celery	1/4 cup	50 mL
Chopped green pepper	1/4 cup	50 mL
Canned tomatoes, mashed	14 oz.	398 mL
Canned okra, sliced, with juice	14 oz.	398 mL
Granulated sugar	1 tsp.	5 mL
Salt	1 tsp.	5 mL
Pepper	1/4 tsp.	1 mL
Garlic powder - or 1 clove, minced	1/4 tsp.	1 mL
Thyme	1/8 tsp.	0.5 mL
Cayenne sprinkle (optional)		
Shrimp, or crab, or some of both	4 - 6 cups	1 - 1.5 L
Hot cooked rice	2 cups	500 mL
Green onions, sliced (optional)	2	2

First make a brown roux (roo) by stirring flour and margarine together in heavy large saucepan over medium heat until dark brown, the color of chocolate. This will take quite a few minutes. Do not scorch.

As soon as desired color is reached, stir in onion to reduce temperature and stop the browning. Add water, celery, green pepper, tomatoes, okra, sugar, salt, pepper, garlic powder and thyme. Sprinkle with cayenne. The amount depends on how hot you want it. Bring to boil. Cover and simmer 30 to 45 minutes or longer, stirring occasionally.

Add shrimp and crab. Tuna may be added for bulk and economy. Add enough seafood to make it thick.

Place mound of rice in each bowl. Sprinkle with green onion. Ladle soup into bowls. Serve New Orleans style with Gumbo Filé on the side if desired. Serve with thick slices of garlic bread or crusty rolls. Makes about 6 cups (1.5 L).

OXTAIL SOUP

Make the first part of this a day ahead. Chill overnight then discard top layer of fat. The end result is an extremely rich-looking-tasting soup. Looks long and difficult but it isn't.

FIRST DAY

Oxtail, cut at joints	1	1
Butter or margarine	2 tbsp.	30 mL
Medium onions, chopped	2	2
Water	5 cups	1.1 L
Beef bouillon cubes - ¹/₅ oz. (6 g) size	2	2
Salt	1 tsp.	5 mL
Pepper	¹/₄ tsp.	1 mL
Whole cloves	2	2
Bay leaf	1	1

SECOND DAY

Butter or margarine	¹/₄ cup	50 mL
All-purpose flour	¹/₄ cup	50 mL
Previously prepared meaty stock		
Water	5 cups	1.1 L
Canned tomato paste	5¹/₂ oz.	156 mL
Vinegar	1 tsp.	5 mL
Granulated sugar	1 tsp.	5 mL
Thinly sliced carrot	1 cup	250 mL
Sliced celery	1 cup	250 mL
Diced turnip	1 cup	250 mL
Pearl or pot barley	¹/₄ cup	50 mL

First Day: Brown oxtail in butter in large pot.

Add onion and brown.

Add water, beef cubes, salt, pepper, cloves and bay leaf. Bring to boil. Cover and simmer for 2 hours. Skim as needed. Discard bay leaf and cloves. Remove bones. Cut up meat and return to broth. Pour into container to chill in refrigerator.

(continued on next page)

Second Day: Put butter and flour into large pot. Stir and brown until color of dull copper penny.

Discard layer of fat from meaty stock. Add stock to butter and flour mixture in pot. Add water, tomato paste, vinegar and sugar. Add carrot, celery, turnip, barley. Bring to boil. Cover and simmer until vegetables and barley are cooked, about 1½ hours. Add more water if necessary. Makes about 13 cups (3 L).

Variation: Add soy sauce to taste, up to 3 tbsp. (50 mL).

BEEF NOODLE SOUP

Complete with tomatoes and vegetables. A good meal. May be halved. Freezes well.

Meaty beef soupbone	1½ lbs.	700 g
Water	7 cups	1.5 L
Salt	1 tbsp.	15 mL
Pepper	½ tsp.	2 mL
Canned tomatoes, mashed	28 oz.	796 mL
Sliced carrot	½ cup	125 mL
Sliced onion	½ cup	125 mL
Sliced celery	¼ cup	50 mL
Parsley flakes	1 tsp.	5 mL
Granulated sugar	½ tsp.	2 mL
Egg noodles or broken spaghetti or vermicelli	2 cups	500 mL

Put soupbone, water, salt and pepper into pot. Bring to boil. Cover and simmer for 1½ to 2 hours. Skim if needed. Remove meat from bone. Cut into bite size pieces or smaller. Return to stock. Discard bone.

Add next 6 ingredients. Simmer for 20 minutes.

Add noodles and simmer for 7 minutes more. Makes about 20 cups (5 L).

Pictured on page 89.

CABBAGE SOUP

A hearty soup, full of flavor. Contains tomato juice.

Ground beef (lean)	1/2 lb.	250 g
Finely chopped onion	1/4 cup	50 mL
Condensed beef broth	10 oz.	284 mL
Tomato juice	4 cups	1 L
Water	1 cup	250 mL
Salt	3/4 tsp.	3 mL
Pepper	1/4 tsp.	1 mL
Garlic powder	1/8 tsp.	0.5 mL
Granulated sugar	1/2 tsp.	2 mL
Shredded cabbage, packed	5 cups	1.25 L

Scramble-fry ground beef in frying pan until brown.

Put next 9 ingredients into large pot. Add ground beef. Bring to a boil. Cover and simmer about 30 minutes. Serve. Makes about 8 cups (1.75 L).

NAVY BEAN SOUP

Good flavor with lots of body.

Water	10 cups	2.5 L
Chicken bouillon cubes - 1/5 oz. (6 g) size	3	3
Dried white beans	2 cups	500 mL
Salt pork (or ham hock)	1 lb.	450 g
Bay leaf	1	1
Medium onion, chopped	1	1
Diced celery	1/2 cup	125 mL

(continued on next page)

Combine water and chicken cubes in large pot. Bring to boil over medium heat. Stir to dissolve cubes.

Add beans, pork and bay leaf. Simmer, covered, until beans are tender, about 2 hours. Stir occasionally. Discard bay leaf. Remove meat and cut into small pieces. Return meat to pot.

Add onion and celery. Continue to cook until vegetables are tender. Serve hot. Makes about 8 cups (1.75 L).

TOMATO ZUCCHINI SOUP

A garden soup with a good, mild flavor. Touches of green in the red soup add interest in texture and color. Excellent.

Butter or margarine	2 tbsp.	30 mL
Sliced onion	2 cups	500 mL
Chicken stock, page 101	4 cups	1 L
Cubed zucchini	8 cups	2 L
Large tomatoes, peeled, cut in chunks	5	5
Fresh parsley, chopped	1 tbsp.	15 mL
Oregano	1/4 tsp.	1 mL
Basil	1/4 tsp.	1 mL
Dry dill weed	1/4 tsp.	1 mL
Celery flakes	1/2 tsp.	2 mL
Granulated sugar	1 tsp.	5 mL
Salt	1/2 tsp.	2 mL

Put butter and onion into large soup pot. Sauté until soft and clear.

Add remaining ingredients. Bring to boil. Cover and simmer for 20 minutes. Check for seasoning. Makes about 10 cups (2.25 L).

Note: To peel tomatoes, immerse in boiling water for 1 minute, then peel.

Pictured on cover.

CONDENSED TOMATO SOUP

Great for a good tomato crop. Makes a condensed soup to freeze or bottle. Flavor is similar to commercial variety.

Ripe tomatoes, quartered or cut up	7½ lbs.	3.5 kg
Medium onions, cut in chunks	3	3
Celery ribs, chopped	6	6
Whole cloves	4	4
Bay leaf	1	1
Sprigs of parsley	6	6
Butter or margarine	½ cup	125 mL
All-purpose flour	6 tbsp.	100 mL
Granulated sugar	¼ cup	50 mL
Salt	2 tbsp.	30 mL
Cayenne pepper	⅛ tsp.	0.5 mL

Combine first 6 ingredients in large saucepan. Bring to boil. Tomatoes will make enough liquid as they boil. Cover and simmer on low heat for 2 hours. Discard bay leaf and cloves. Force the rest through cone ricer or run through blender, then strain to remove seeds.

Melt butter in saucepan. Stir in remaining ingredients. Add some strained soup and mix. Pour back into soup. Boil and stir until thickened. Pour into hot sterilized jars to within 1 inch (2.5 cm) of top. Place sterilized metal lids on jars and screw metal bands on securely and process 20 minutes in water bath or freeze in small containers. Makes about 9 cups condensed soup.

To serve, add pinch of baking soda to 1 cup (250 mL) hot tomato soup, then add 1 cup (250 mL) hot milk.

TOMATO SOUP AU GRATIN

This rivals French Onion Soup for goodness. Although a good sized recipe, it can easily be halved. Puffed Lids, page 12 make this most impressive.

Butter or margarine	¼ cup	50 mL
Sliced onion	4 cups	900 mL
All-purpose flour	2 tbsp.	30 mL
Salt	1½ tsp.	7 mL
Pepper	¼ tsp.	1 mL
Condensed beef broth	20 oz.	568 mL
Water	2 cups	450 mL
Canned tomatoes	28 oz.	796 mL
Granulated sugar	½ tsp.	2 mL
French bread slices, toasted	6 - 8	6 - 8
Grated Cheddar cheese	2 cups	500 mL

Put butter and onion into large saucepan. Sauté until onion is golden brown.

Mix in flour, salt and pepper. Add beef broth and water. Stir until it boils and thickens.

Run tomatoes and sugar through blender. Add to saucepan. Bring to boil again. Cover and simmer 15 minutes. Ladle into broiler-proof bowls. Makes about 10 cups (2.25 L).

Cut corners off toast if necessary. Put 1 slice on top of soup. Sprinkle generously with cheese. Broil to melt.

Pare Pointer

If your stomach gets sunburned, you have a pot roast.

TOMATO RICE SOUP

The secret ingredient is citric acid — not a necessity but worth buying at your local drugstore for this recipe alone.

Water	6 cups	1.5 L
Condensed tomato soup	20 oz.	598 mL
Canned tomato paste	5½ oz.	156 mL
Cooked rice	1½ cups	375 mL
Seasoned salt	1 tsp.	5 mL
Pepper	½ tsp.	2 mL
Parsley flakes	1 tsp.	5 mL
Citric acid	¼ tsp.	1 mL

Combine all ingredients in large saucepan. Simmer together for 5 minutes. Makes 4½ cups (1 L).

Variation: Use some milk in place of the water for a creamed look.

Pictured on page 125.

CHICKEN NOODLE SOUP

Lots of noodles in this soup.

Chicken stock, page 101	4 cups	1 L
Noodles (see note)	2 oz.	57 g
Cooked chicken, diced or shredded	½ cup	125 mL
Parsley flakes	½ tsp.	125 mL

Combine all together in saucepan. Simmer until noodles are cooked. Makes a scant 4 cups (750 mL).

Note: Noodle amount is all you can hold in 1 hand, a big handful.

Pictured on page 125.

CHICKEN RICE SOUP: Omit noodles. Add 1 cup (250 mL) minute rice. Simmer to cook, stirring often.

CHICKEN AND STARS: Omit noodles. Add ½ cup (125 mL) pasta stars. Simmer until cooked. Stir often.

GREEN BEAN SOUP

Bright and colorful as well as tasty. Cooks in no time.

Chicken stock, page 101	5 cups	1.25 L
Green string beans, fresh or frozen, cut in short pieces - or 28 oz. (796 mL) canned	4 cups	1 L
Finely chopped onion	1/4 cup	50 mL
Diced celery	2 tbsp.	30 mL
Medium carrots, diced or sliced	2	2
Salt	1 tsp.	5 mL
Pepper	1/4 tsp.	1 mL
Sliced pepperoni, smokies, or other processed sausage	1 cup	250 mL
Cheddar cheese for garnish		

Combine all ingredients except cheese in large pot. Bring to a boil and simmer, covered, for about 20 minutes. Serve with grated Cheddar cheese as a garnish in center of each bowl. Makes about 6 cups (1.3 L).

Note: If you don't have chicken stock on hand make it easily using 5 cups (1.25 L) water and 5 chicken bouillon cubes - 1/5 oz. (6 g) size.

TOMATO SPICE SOUP

Good looking soup with flavor to match. Easily halved.

Medium onions, coarsely chopped	2	2
Garlic cloves	2	2
Butter or margarine	1/4 cup	50 mL
Ripe tomatoes, coarsely chopped, (about 10)	4 lbs.	2 kg
Chicken stock, page 101	6 cups	1.25 L
Canned tomato paste	4 tbsp.	60 mL
Salt	1 1/2 tsp.	7 mL
White pepper	1/2 - 1 tsp.	2 - 5 mL
Sweet basil	2 tbsp.	30 mL
Granulated sugar	2 tsp.	10 mL

Measure all ingredients into large soup pot. Bring to boil. Cover and simmer slowly for 15 minutes, stirring often. Cool a bit and run through blender. Strain to remove seeds if desired. Check for seasoning. Makes about 13 cups (3 L).

SAUERKRAUT SOUP

A good color as well as a great flavor. May also be made without caraway seed if desired.

Sauerkraut, drained and rinsed	14 oz.	398 mL
Beef stock, page 102	8 cups	1.8 L
Medium onion, chopped	1	1
Apple, peeled and grated	1	1
Canned tomato paste	5½ oz.	156 mL
Paprika	1 tsp.	5 mL
Caraway seed	1 tsp.	5 mL

Combine all ingredients in large pot. Bring to boil. Cover and simmer for 45 minutes. Makes about 8 cups (1.8 L).

MEATY SAUERKRAUT SOUP: Omit caraway seed. Add 4 slices bacon, fried crispy and crumbled. Add about 1 cup (250 mL) smoked sausage, knockwurst, beer sausage or frankfurters, cut into small pieces. This makes a different and delicious soup.

ZUCCHINI SOUP

This is thick with good color from the peelings. May also be served cold.

Zucchini, sliced, unpeeled	2 lbs.	1 kg
Medium onion, sliced	1	1
Garlic clove, minced	1	1
Butter or margarine	1 tbsp.	15 mL
Hot water	2 cups	500 mL
Chicken bouillon cubes - ⅕ oz. (6 g) size	2	2
Lemon juice	½ tsp.	2 mL
Salt	1 tsp.	5 mL
Chopped chives	1 tbsp.	15 mL

(continued on next page)

Combine zucchini, onion, garlic, and butter in frying pan. Sauté slowly while covered (to steam-fry) until soft, about 10 minutes.

Add water, chicken bouillon cubes, lemon juice and salt. Run through blender. Return to saucepan. Heat.

Stir in chives. Serve hot. Makes about 5½ cups (1.2 L).

Variation: Add 1/2 tsp. (2 mL) curry powder.

CHICKEN LENTIL SOUP

It is better to stew the chicken; chill overnight and complete the next day. Good for what ails you! Freezes well.

Stewing chicken	3 - 3¼ lbs.	1.5 kg
Water to cover, at least	12 cups	3 L
Salt	5 tsp.	25 mL
Pepper	½ tsp.	2 mL
Pearl or pot barley	½ cup	125mL
Medium potatoes, cubed	2	2
Medium carrots, sliced	3	3
Large onion, chopped	1	1
Chopped celery	1 cup	250 mL
Dry vegetable soup mix	½ cup	125 mL
Red lentils	½ cup	125 mL
Poultry seasoning (to taste)	¾ tsp.	4 mL

Put chicken, water, salt and pepper in large pot. Bring to boil. Cover and simmer for 2 to 2½ hours. Add boiling water as needed to keep water level up. Remove chicken from stock. Cut meat into small pieces and return to stock. Chill.

Remove and discard fat. Heat to boil. Add remaining ingredients. Return to boil. Cover and simmer for 2 hours. Check for seasoning. Makes about 20 cups (4.5 L).

Note: Chicken carcass may be used as well as chicken backs and necks. Stock may need to be strengthened with chicken bouillon cubes.

CHILI CHEESE SOUP

Cheese soup with a new twist. Spicy and delectable. Brownish color.

Butter or margarine	2 tbsp.	30 mL
All-purpose flour	1 tbsp.	15 mL
Beef stock, page 102	4 cups	1 L
Canned tomatoes, mashed	14 oz.	398 mL
Finely chopped onion	1 cup	250 mL
Chili powder	2 tsp.	10 mL
Dry mustard powder	1/2 tsp.	2 mL
Paprika	1/2 tsp.	2 mL
Grated Monterey Jack cheese	2 cups	500 mL
Chives or parsley for garnish		

Melt butter in saucepan. Stir in flour. Add stock, stirring, until it boils and thickens.

Add tomatoes, onion, chili powder, mustard and paprika. Bring to boil. Cover and simmer 20 minutes.

Add cheese. Stir to melt. Garnish with chopped chives or chopped parsley. Makes about 6 cups (1.3 L).

TOMATO PASTA SOUP

So easy to prepare. Tastes like it took ages to make.

Beef stock, page 102	2 cups	500 mL
Chicken stock, page 101	2 cups	500 mL
Tomato juice	2 cups	500 mL
Water	1 cup	250 mL
Elbow macaroni	1 cup	250 mL
Salt	1/2 tsp.	3 mL
Pepper	1/8 tsp.	0.5 mL

Put all together in large saucepan. Bring to boil, stirring occasionally. Boil for 7 minutes until macaroni is cooked. Makes about 6 cups (1.3 L).

Pictured on page 89.

Even made from scratch, this is quick and appetizing. Try serving with Puffed Lids, page 12, for a dazzling look.

Medium Spanish onions	4	4
Butter or margarine	¼ cup	50 mL
Beef bouillon cubes - ⅕ oz.(6 g) size	6	6
Water	6 cups	1.35 L
Salt	1½ tsp.	7 mL

French bread slices, toasted, or
croutons
Grated Parmesan or Mozzarella cheese

Cut peeled onions in half lengthwise. Slice into thin slices. Cut any long slices in half. Sauté in butter in frying pan until a rich brown color. This is easier to do in batches.

Combine beef cubes, water and salt in large pot. Heat. Stir to dissolve cubes. Add browned onion. Simmer to distribute flavor and to finish cooking onion. Ladle into bowls.

Top with toasted slices of French bread or croutons. Cover with lots of cheese. Bake in 450°F (230°C) oven or broil to melt and brown cheese. If bowls aren't ovenproof, broil cheese-covered toast sepa–rately. Place on soup to serve.

RED ONION SOUP: Substitute red onions for the white. Makes a delicious variation.

The safest way to raise cane is to plant sugar cubes.

CORN CHOWDER

A can of soup shortens the sauce-making procedure. A great chowder.

Bacon slices, diced	4	4
Medium onion, sliced or chopped	1	1
Niblet corn, frozen, fresh or 10 oz. (284 g) canned cream corn	2 cups	500 mL
Diced raw potato	1½ cups	375 mL
Condensed cream of mushroom soup	10 oz.	284 mL
Milk	3 cups	750 mL
Salt	½ tsp.	2 mL
Pepper	⅛ tsp.	0.5 mL

Put bacon and onion into large pot. Sauté together until onion is clear and limp.

Add next 6 ingredients. Bring to boil. Cover and simmer until potato is cooked. Stir occasionally. Makes about 6 cups (1.3 L).

TOMATO MACARONI SOUP

A tasty combination with a rich dark color for eye appeal.

Beef bouillon cubes - ⅕ oz. (6 g) size	4	4
Water	5 cups	1.25 L
Sliced carrot	1 cup	250 mL
Chopped onion	1 cup	250 mL
Chopped turnip	½ cup	125 mL
Canned tomatoes	14 oz.	398 mL
Macaroni	½ cup	125 mL
Salt	1 tsp.	5 mL
Pepper	⅛ tsp.	0.5 mL

Dissolve bouillon cubes in water in large saucepan over medium heat. Add carrot, onion, turnip and tomatoes. Bring to boil. Cover and simmer about 20 minutes to cook vegetables.

Add macaroni, salt and pepper. Continue to cook for about 7 minutes to cook macaroni. Makes a generous 6 cups (1.5 L).

PEA SOUP

Made from split green peas. Good choice for a pea soup. Good color.
Excellent taste. Freezes well.

Ham bone	1	1
Water	12 cups	2.75 L
Split green peas	3 cups	700 mL
Medium carrots, shredded	3	3
Medium onion, chopped	1	1
Salt	2 tsp.	10 mL
Pepper	1/2 tsp.	2 mL
Thyme	1/4 tsp.	1 mL

Bring ham bone and water to boil. Cover and simmer for about 2 hours. Strain. Measure broth. Add water to bring it up to 12 cups (2.75 L).

Add remaining 6 ingredients. Bring to boil. Cover and simmer at least 1 hour. Peas should be soft and getting mushy. May need a bit of water to thin. Makes about 10 cups (2.25 L).

FRESH PEA SOUP

Garden-fresh color, with a hard-to-beat fresh garden flavor.

Chopped onion	1/2 cup	125 mL
Butter or margarine	2 tbsp.	30 mL
All-purpose flour	1/4 cup	60 mL
Chicken stock, page 101	4 cups	1 L
Peas, fresh or frozen	2 1/2 cups	625 mL

Sauté onion in butter until soft and clear. Do not brown.

Add flour. Mix in. Add chicken stock, stirring, until it boils and thick-ens.

Add peas. Simmer for 5 minutes. Run through blender. Return to saucepan until ready to serve. Makes a generous 4 cups (1 L).

SPLIT PEA TURKEY SOUP

Uses yellow peas. Stock may be made from chicken as well. You may substitute leftover turkey with any poultry meats, such as chicken, duck or goose. Freezes well. Recipe may be halved.

Turkey stock, see Chicken stock, page 101	12 cups	2.75 L
Yellow split peas	2 cups	450 mL
Chopped onion	1 cup	250 mL
Thinly sliced carrot	⅔ cup	150 mL
Chopped celery	½ cup	125 mL
Salt	1 tsp.	5 mL
Pepper	½ tsp.	2 mL
Garlic powder	½ tsp.	2 mL
Leftover turkey (or chicken), diced	2 cups	500 mL

Measure first 8 ingredients into large pot. Bring to boil. Cover and simmer about 1 hour until peas are soft and a bit mushy.

Stir in turkey. Heat. Thin with water if necessary. Makes about 10 cups (2.25 L).

CHEDDAR CHOWDER

Serve with a salad and crusty bread for a complete meal.

Diced potato	3 cups	750 mL
Diced onion	1 cup	250 mL
Diced carrot	1½ cups	375 mL
Diced celery	¾ cup	175 mL
Chicken stock, page 101	2 cups	500 mL
Salt	½ tsp.	2 mL
Pepper (white is best)	¼ tsp.	1 mL
Grated Cheddar cheese, old or medium	2 cups	500 mL

Measure first 7 ingredients into saucepan. Bring to boil. Cover and simmer until vegetables are tender. Do not drain.

Stir in cheese until melted. Makes about 5 cups (1.25 L).

CHEESE SOUP: Run tender vegetables and stock through blender. Return to saucepan. Add cheese and melt.

BEER SOUP: Add ½ cup (125 mL) beer, 2 tbsp. (30 mL) Parmesan cheese and ½ tsp. (2 mL) dry mustard to Cheese Soup.

Regular meatballs turn this simple soup into meal-type fare. Freezes.

MEATBALLS

Lean ground beef	**1 lb.**	**450 g**
Dry bread crumbs	**1/3 cup**	**75 mL**
Milk or water	**1/3 cup**	**75 mL**
Onion flakes, crushed	**2 tsp.**	**10 mL**
Worcestershire sauce	**1 tsp.**	**5 mL**
Salt	**2 tsp.**	**10 mL**
Pepper	**1/4 tsp.**	**1 mL**
Garlic salt	**1/2 tsp.**	**2 mL**

SOUP

Beef stock, page 102	**6 cups**	**1.5 L**
Tomato juice	**2 cups**	**500 mL**
Small pasta	**1/2 cup**	**125 mL**
Salt	**1/8 tsp.**	**0.5 mL**

Meatballs: Mix all ingredients together well. Shape into 3/4 inch (2 cm) balls (or smaller). Makes about 2 dozen. Set aside.

Soup: Put all ingredients into large saucepan. Bring to boil. Add meatballs. Return to boil. Cover and simmer slowly for about 7 min– utes until pasta and meatballs are cooked. Makes about 10 cups (2.5 L).

Fare Pointer

Liquid assets to a teenager is a refrigerator full of soft drinks.

VEGETARIAN BEAN SOUP

Easy to make this thick soup. Good flavor. A real meal.

Dried white beans	2 cups	500 mL
Water	12 cups	3 L
Onion, chopped	1	1
Celery ribs, chopped	2	2
Carrot, finely diced	1	1
Canned tomatoes	14 oz.	398 mL
Medium potatoes, peeled and diced	2	2
Salt	2 tsp.	10 mL
Pepper	1/2 tsp.	2 mL
Parsley flakes	1 tsp.	5 mL
Garlic powder	1/4 tsp.	1 mL
Thyme	1/4 tsp.	1 mL

Put beans and water in large pot. Bring to boil. Cover and simmer 1½ to 2 hours until beans are tender.

Add remaining ingredients. Return to boil. Cover and simmer about 15 minutes until vegetables are tender. Add more salt if needed. Serve hot. Makes about 10 cups (2.5 L).

SQUASH SOUP

This is different from Pumpkin Soup. Another winning flavor. Freezes.

Butter or margarine	2 tbsp.	30 mL
Chopped onion	1 cup	250 mL
Chicken stock, page 101	2 cups	500 mL
Cooked yellow squash, mashed	2 cups	500 mL
Canned baby food apple sauce	4½ oz.	128 mL
Salt	1/2 tsp.	2 mL
Pepper	1/8 tsp.	0.5 mL
Sour cream or yogurt for garnish		

(continued on next page)

Put butter and onion into saucepan. Sauté onion until soft and clear.

Add remaining ingredients. Run through blender and return to sauce-pan. Heat through. Garnish with a dab of sour cream or yogurt. Makes about 5 cups (1.1 L).

CURRIED SQUASH SOUP: Add 1 tsp. (5 mL) curry powder. Simmer gently before serving. Excellent addition.

CHEESY HAM CHOWDER

The addition of peas to the blended vegetables gives a distinctive flavor. A fabulous chowder.

Diced potato	2 cups	500 mL
Diced onion	1 cup	250 mL
Diced carrot	1/3 cup	75 mL
Chicken bouillon cube - 1/5 oz.(6 g) size	1	1
Water	1 cup	250 mL
Parsley flakes	1 tsp.	5 mL
Peas, fresh or frozen	3/4 cup	175 mL
Canned flaked ham	6½ oz.	184 g
Milk	2 cups	500 mL
Mild processed cheese, cut up (Velveeta is good)	8 oz.	250 g

Put first 6 ingredients into saucepan. Cook until vegetables are tender. Cool a bit, then run through blender. Transfer back into saucepan.

Add peas, ham, milk and cheese. Heat, stirring often. Gently simmer to cook peas. Makes about 8 cups (1.75 L).

A diamond is a girl's idea of a stepping stone to better things to come.

MEATY SQUASH SOUP

A meal in itself, this soup is outstanding. A large recipe, it freezes well. Scrumptious!

Boneless pork shoulder, cut bite size or smaller	2 lbs.	1 kg
All-purpose flour	1/3 cup	75 mL
Cooking oil	1/4 cup	50 mL
Sliced green onion	1/4 cup	50 mL
Garlic clove, minced	1	1
Sliced celery	3/4 cup	175 mL
Chopped onion	1 cup	250 mL
Hot water	6 cups	1.5 L
Beef bouillon cubes - 1/5 oz.(6 g) size	5	5
Canned tomatoes	28 oz.	796 mL
Yellow squash, peeled and cubed or sliced, 2 medium	10 cups	2.25 L
Parsley flakes	1 tbsp.	15 mL
Granulated sugar	1 tsp.	5 mL
Salt	1 tsp.	5 mL
Pepper	1/2 tsp.	2 mL

Put meat and flour in bag. Shake to thoroughly dredge.

Put oil in large soup pot. Add meat and brown.

Add next 4 ingredients. Sauté until onion is soft and clear.

Stir hot water and bouillon cubes together until dissolved. Add to pot. Add remaining ingredients. Bring to boil. Cover and simmer about 1 to 1½ hours. Check for seasoning. More water will probably be needed to thin. Makes about 16 cups (3.6 L).

The harried parents of quadruplets exclaimed "Four crying out loud!"

BEEF BARLEY SOUP

A meaty soup guaranteed to please every appetite. Freeze portion size for a continuing supply. Extra good. Use leftover roast beef.

Water	6 cups	1.5 L
Beef bouillon cubes - 1/5 oz.(6 g) size	6	6
Canned tomatoes, mashed	28 oz.	796 mL
Condensed tomato soup	10 oz.	284 mL
Shredded carrot	2 cups	500 mL
Shredded potato	2 cups	500 mL
Chopped onion	1½ cups	375 mL
Chopped celery	1 cup	250 mL
Pearl or pot barley	½ cup	125 mL
Water	6 cups	1.5 L
Parsley flakes	1 tbsp.	15 mL
Granulated sugar	1 tsp.	5 mL
Salt	1 tsp.	5 mL
Pepper	¼ tsp.	1 mL
Thyme	¼ tsp.	1 mL
Cooked roast beef, chopped	3 cups	750 mL

Heat first amount of water and bouillon cubes in large pot. Stir to dissolve.

Add remaining ingredients except beef. Bring to boil. Cover and simmer slowly for about 1½ hours.

Add beef and simmer ½ hour more. Makes about 22 cups (5 L).

HAMBURGER SOUP: Omit chopped roast beef. Scramble-fry 2 lbs. (1 kg) lean ground beef. Add to soup half way through cooking. Part ground beef and part roast beef may be used also.

His excuse to the policeman was that he stole the budgie for a lark.

TOMATO VEGETABLE SOUP

Good and thick with vegetables for added interest.

Butter or margarine	3 tbsp.	50 mL
Diced onion	1 cup	250 mL
Diced potato	½ cup	125 mL
Diced carrot	½ cup	125 mL
All-purpose flour	3 tbsp.	60 mL
Salt	½ tsp.	2 mL
Pepper	¼ tsp.	1 mL
Chicken stock, page 101	2 cups	500 mL
Canned tomatoes, mashed	14 oz.	398 mL
Granulated sugar	1 tsp.	5 mL
Cream or rich milk	½ cup	125 mL

Put butter, onion, potato and carrot into saucepan. Sauté until onion is clear and soft.

Mix in flour, salt and pepper. Add chicken stock. Stir until it boils and thickens. Simmer 10 minutes.

Add tomatoes and sugar. Heat through.

Stir in cream. Do not boil. Makes about 4 cups (900 mL).

BACON AND BEAN SOUP

Pork and beans never tasted so good.

Bacon slices, cut up small	3	3
Finely chopped onion	½ cup	125 mL
Boiling water	1 cup	250 mL
Chicken bouillon cube - ⅕ oz.(6 g) size	1	1
Beans in tomato sauce	14 oz.	398 mL
Dry celery flakes	½ tsp.	2 mL

Combine bacon with onion in large saucepan. Fry slowly until onion is clear and soft.

Add water and chicken cube. Stir until dissolved.

Stir in beans and celery flakes. Simmer gently, covered, for about 15 minutes. This is quite a thick soup so more water may be added at this point if desired. Serve hot. Makes a scant 3 cups (750 mL).

LENTIL SOUP

Thick and nourishing. Color of lentils determines color of soup. The red ones make a more attractive color.

Chicken stock, page 101	8 cups	2 L
Lentils, red or brown	2 cups	500 mL
Medium onions, chopped	2	2
Medium carrots, cut up	2	2
Medium potato, cut up	1	1
Garlic powder (or 1 clove, minced)	¼ tsp.	1 mL
Salt	½ tsp.	2 mL
Pepper	¼ tsp.	1 mL

Combine all ingredients in large pot. Be sure to rinse lentils well. Bring to a boil, stirring often. Cover and simmer for about 45 minutes. Stir occasionally. Makes about 9 cups (2 L).

Variation: May be made with ham stock including small pieces of ham, or simply add 5 oz. (142 g) canned flaked ham.

CREAM OF SHRIMP SOUP

Medium-thick with good color and flavor to match. Freezes.

Butter or margarine	3 tbsp.	50 mL
Chopped onion	3 tbsp.	50 mL
Chopped celery	2 tbsp.	30 mL
All-purpose flour	3 tbsp.	50 mL
Salt	½ tsp.	2 mL
Pepper	¼ tsp.	1 mL
Chicken stock, page 101	2 cups	500 mL
Milk	1 cup	250 mL
Small frozen shrimp, chopped	1¼ cups	300 mL

Put butter, onion and celery into saucepan. Sauté until onion is soft and clear.

Mix in flour, salt and pepper. Add chicken stock and milk. Cook and stir until it boils and thickens.

Add shrimp. Simmer until hot or about 5 minutes if shrimp is raw. Makes about 3½ cups (800 mL).

SCALLOP CHOWDER

Scallops with their own delicate flavor.

Fish stock, page 100, or packaged	2 cups	500 mL
Milk	3¾ cups	850 mL
Diced potato	1 cup	250 mL
Onion salt	¼ tsp.	1 mL
Scallops, fresh or frozen, cut into pieces	1 lb.	455 g
All-purpose flour	2 tbsp.	30 mL
Milk	¼ cup	50 mL
Paprika or green onion for garnish		

(continued on next page)

Measure fish stock, first amount of milk, potato, and onion salt into large saucepan. Bring to boil. Cover and simmer until potato is cooked.

Add scallops. Simmer 5 minutes to cook.

Mix flour and second amount of milk until no lumps remain. Stir into simmering soup to thicken. Garnish with paprika or sliced green onion. Makes about 6 cups (1.3 L).

LOBSTER CHOWDER

Chock full of goodness. Very good. An expensive seafood stretches well this way.

Medium potatoes, diced	2	2
Medium onion, diced	1	1
Water	1 cup	250 mL
Milk	1 1/2 cups	350 mL
Light cream	1 cup	200 mL
Salt	1 tsp.	5 mL
Pepper	1/4 tsp.	1 mL
Canned lobster, cartilage removed	5 oz.	142 g
Butter	2 tbsp.	30 mL
Milk	1/2 cup	125 mL
All-purpose flour	3 tbsp.	50 mL

Bring potato and onion to a boil in water. Simmer, covered, until cooked. Do not drain.

Add next 6 ingredients. An additional 5 oz. (142 g) of lobster may be added if desired. Bring to a simmer.

Mix second amount of milk into flour until no lumps remain. Stir into simmering soup to thicken. Serve hot. Makes about 7 cups (1.6 L).

Pictured on page 143.

Pare Pointer

Hippies study stars because they're so far out.

CRAB CHOWDER

One of the most economical crab recipes. It stretches a long way.

Bacon slices, diced	3	3
Chopped onion	1/2 cup	125 mL
Water	2 cups	500 mL
Diced potato	2 cups	500 mL
Canned tomatoes, mashed	14 oz.	398 mL
Lemon juice	1/2 tsp.	2 mL
Bay leaf	1	1
Canned crab, cartilage removed	5 oz.	142 g
- or 1 cup (250 mL) fresh		
Milk	2 cups	500 mL
Salt	1 tsp.	5 mL
Pepper	1/2 tsp.	2 mL
Instant potato flakes	1/4 cup	60 mL

Sauté bacon and onion in large saucepan until onion is soft and clear.

Add water, potato, tomatoes, lemon juice and bay leaf. Bring to boil. Cover and simmer to cook potato, about 10 minutes. Discard bay leaf.

Stir in remaining ingredients. Heat. Add more potato flakes if not thick enough. Also good blended. Makes about 8 cups (2 L).

OYSTER SOUP

A family favorite from the Maritimes where the eastern oysters are small and among the mildest. Very quick to prepare.

Milk	4 cups	900 mL
Soda cracker crumbs	1/2 cup	125 mL
Salt	1 tsp.	5 mL
Pepper	1/4 tsp.	1 mL
Small oysters with juice (about 24),	2 cups	450 mL
fresh, frozen or canned		
Butter or margarine	1 tbsp.	15 mL

(continued on next page)

Combine milk, cracker crumbs, salt and pepper in saucepan. Heat to boiling point.

Add oysters with juice and butter. Bring to boil again and simmer until edges of oysters curl, about 5 minutes. Makes about 4½ cups (1 L).

NEPTUNE CHOWDER

A cheese-flavored fish soup. Try it with or without any fishing luck. This is good without adding any cheese at all and is super if double the amount is added. Freezes well.

Butter or margarine	2 tbsp.	30 mL
Thinly sliced onion	2 cups	500 mL
Chopped celery	1 cup	250 mL
Diced potato	2 cups	500 mL
Sliced carrot	1 cup	250 mL
Water	2 cups	500 mL
Salt	1 tsp.	5 mL
Pepper	¼ tsp.	1 mL
Fish fillets, fresh or frozen, cut bite size	1 lb.	454 g
Milk	2 cups	500 mL
Mild process cheese (Velveeta is good)	4 oz.	125 g
Chives or parsley for garnish		

Put butter, onion and celery into large saucepan. Sauté until onion is clear and soft.

Add potato, carrot, water, salt and pepper. Bring to boil. Cover and simmer about 10 minutes.

Add fish and simmer 10 minutes more.

Add milk and cheese. Heat, stirring often, until cheese melts. Do not boil. Season to taste. Garnish with chopped chives or parsley. Makes about 8½ cups (2 L).

Pictured on page 143.

MOCK OYSTER SOUP

The taste resemblance is amazing. Easy and scrumptious.

Butter or margarine	2 tbsp.	30 mL
All-purpose flour	2 tbsp.	30 mL
Milk	1 cup	250 mL
Milk	3 cups	650 mL
Soda cracker crumbs	1/4 cup	60 mL
Canned tuna, drained	6 1/2 oz.	184 g
Salt	1/2 tsp.	2 mL
Pepper	1/4 tsp.	1 mL
Celery flakes	1/2 tsp.	2 mL
Onion powder	1/4 tsp.	1 mL

Melt butter in large saucepan. Mix in flour. Add milk. Stir until it boils and thickens.

Add remaining 7 ingredients. Simmer for a few minutes to blend flavors. Makes about 4 cups (900 mL).

CATCH OF THE DAY SOUP

Dark and delicious. It looks similar to beef stew. Easy to double recipe. Whatever your catch — try it!

Medium onion, chopped	1	1
Garlic clove, minced	1	1
Butter or margarine	2 tbsp.	30 mL
Fish fillets, cut in bite size pieces	1/2 lb.	225 g
Canned tomatoes, cut up	14 oz.	398 mL
Water	2 cups	500 mL
Beef bouillon cubes - 1/5 oz.(6 g) size	3	3
Ketchup	1 tbsp.	15 mL
Salt	1/2 tsp.	2 mL
Thyme	1/8 tsp.	0.5 mL

(continued on next page)

Put onion, garlic and butter in large saucepan. Sauté until onion is soft and clear.

Add fish, tomatoes, water, bouillon cubes, ketchup, salt and thyme. Bring to boil. Cover and simmer approximately 10 minutes. Makes about 4⅔ cups (1 L).

TUNA BISQUE

This can't be beaten for economy and flavor. You will think you are eating lobster, it is so good.

Chicken stock, page 101	2 cups	500 mL
Medium onion, chopped	1	1
Medium potato, chopped	1	1
Chopped celery	⅓ cup	75 mL
Diced carrot	⅓ cup	75 mL
Canned tomatoes, mashed	14 oz.	398 mL
Salt	1 tsp.	5 mL
Pepper	¼ tsp.	1 mL
Granulated sugar	1 tsp.	2 mL
Milk	2½ cups	600 mL
Milk	½ cup	125 mL
All-purpose flour	¼ cup	50 mL
Canned tuna with juice	6½ oz.	184 g

Combine first 10 ingredients in large saucepan. Bring to a boil over medium heat. Cover and simmer until vegetables are tender.

Mix second amount of milk and flour together until no lumps remain. Stir into simmering soup to thicken.

Add tuna and juice, breaking it up if necessary. Serve hot. Makes about 8 cups (1.75 L).

Snap! Crackle! Pop! It's a firefly with a short circuit.

MANHATTAN CLAM CHOWDER

Red, robust and hearty. Freezes well.

Bacon slices, diced	3	3
Finely chopped onion	1 cup	250 mL
Finely chopped celery	1 cup	250 mL
Canned minced clams	10 oz.	284 g
Water	3 cups	750 mL
Clam juice	1/2 cup	125 mL
Canned tomatoes, broken up	14 oz.	398 mL
Diced potato	2 cups	500 mL
Diced carrot	1 cup	250 mL
Salt	1 1/2 tsp.	7 mL
Pepper	1/8 tsp.	0.5 mL
Thyme	1/4 tsp.	1 mL
All-purpose flour	2 tbsp.	30 mL
Water	1/4 cup	50 mL

Sauté bacon, onion and celery in large saucepan until tender.

Drain clams, reserving juice. Set aside.

Add next 8 ingredients to bacon mixture in saucepan. Bring to boil. Cover and simmer 30 minutes.

Whisk flour and second amount of water together until smooth. Stir into simmering soup until it thickens. Add clams. Heat. Makes about 8 cups (2 L).

MANHATTAN FISH CHOWDER: Use 1 lb. (454 g) of your favorite fish fillets cut into bite size pieces. Add during last 10 minutes of cooking.

Perhaps a myth is a female moth.

Creamy thick chowder with bright bits of carrot perking up the color. Can easily be doubled or halved. To freeze, omit white sauce and potato.

Finely diced celery	**1 cup**	**250 mL**
Finely diced carrot	**1 cup**	**250 mL**
Finely diced onion	**1 cup**	**250 mL**
Diced potato	**1 cup**	**250 mL**
Water	**2 cups**	**500 mL**
Milk	**7 cups**	**1.75 L**
Butter or margarine, melted	**1 cup**	**250 mL**
All-purpose flour	**1 cup**	**250 mL**
Salt	**2 tsp.**	**10 mL**
Pepper	**1 tsp.**	**5 mL**
Milk	**1 cup**	**250 mL**
Canned baby clams with juice	**10 oz.**	**284 g**
Parsley for garnish		

Put first 5 ingredients into large pot. Simmer, covered, until tender. Do not drain.

In large heavy saucepan, heat first amount of milk.

Stir butter, flour, salt and pepper together well in bowl. Whisk in second amount of milk until smooth. Pour into hot milk and stir until it boils and thickens. Add vegetables with liquid.

Stir in clams with juice. An additional 5 oz. (142 g) of clams with juice may be added if you wish. Heat through. Garnish with fresh chopped parsley. Makes about 12 cups (3 L).

When grapes worry, they wrinkle and turn into raisins.

EASY CLAM CHOWDER

Have this cooking while preparing other things. Requires no watch-ing. Just keep enough water in the double boiler. Rich and thick.

Medium potatoes, diced	2	2
Medium onion, chopped	1	1
Baby clams with juice	5 oz.	142 g
Salt	1/2 tsp.	2 mL
Pepper	1/4 tsp.	1 mL
Evaporated milk	14 oz.	385 mL
Butter or margarine	1 tsp.	5 mL

Put potato and onion in top of double boiler. Add clam juice. Chop clams and add along with salt and pepper. Cover. Cook over boiling water for about 1 1/4 hours or until vegetables are cooked.

Add milk and butter. Continue cooking until heated through. Makes about 4 cups (900 mL).

FISH STOCK

Although food stores now carry instant seafood stock, you may want to make your own. Freezes well.

Water	8 cups	2 L
Onion, coarsely chopped	1	1
Carrots, coarsely chopped	2	2
Celery ribs, coarsely chopped	3	3
Parsley flakes	1 tsp.	5 mL
Bay leaf	1	1
Lemon juice	1 tsp.	5 mL
Fish pieces (bones, heads, tails or whole fish, cleaned and cut up)	1 lb.	500 g
Salt	1 tsp.	5 mL
Pepper	1/4 tsp.	1 mL

Combine all ingredients together in large pot. Bring to boil. Cover and boil slowly for 45 minutes. Strain. Makes about 6 cups (1.4 L).

There is nothing quite like making your own stock. Keep on hand in the freezer.

Chicken (see note)	3½ lbs.	1.5 kg
Water to cover, approximately	14 cups	3.5 L
Chopped onion	1½ cups	375 mL
Medium carrots, cut up	2	2
Chopped celery	¾ cup	150 mL
Parsley flakes	1 tsp.	5 mL
Salt	1 tsp.	5 mL
Pepper	¼ tsp.	1 mL
Bay leaf (optional)	1	1
Thyme	¼ tsp.	1 mL
Whole clove	1	1

Put all ingredients into pot. Bring to boil. Cover and simmer about 2½ hours. Skim as needed. Strain. Remove meat from bones and save for soup or sandwiches. Strain and chill stock. Remove and discard layer of fat before using. Makes about 10 cups (2.25 L).

Note: Fowl, such as a hen, gives maximum flavor. Frying chicken or the equivalent weight in chicken parts may be used. Necks and backs can be stored in the freezer until enough have accumulated. The addition of 4 chicken bouillon cubes will strengthen stock made from younger chickens. Stock may be boiled, uncovered, until reduced in quantity thus making it stronger. A turkey or chicken carcass can also be used to make stock. It helps to brown carcass bones in 450°F (230°C) oven before boiling.Chicken bouillon cubes added to the water will enhance flavor.

QUICK CHICKEN STOCK I: Dilute condensed chicken broth as directed on can and use according to recipe.

QUICK CHICKEN STOCK II: Dissolve chicken bouillon cubes according to package directions and use as directed in recipe.

BASIC BEEF STOCK

This is the first step to delicious soups. Start from scratch. Stock freezes well.

Ingredient	Imperial	Metric
Beef soup bones	2 - 3 lbs.	1 - 1.25 kg
Onions, quartered	2	2
Carrots, quartered	2	2
Celery stalks, cut	2	2
Bay leaf, small	1	1
Thyme	$1/4$ tsp.	1 mL
Whole cloves	2	2
Parsley flakes	1 tsp.	5 mL
Salt	1 tsp.	5 mL
Peppercorns	4	4
Water	10 cups	2.25 L

Put all ingredients into large pot. Bring to boil. Cover and simmer for about 2½ hours, adding more water to maintain water level as needed. Skim if necessary. Strain. Remove meat from bones. Chop and save for soup or sandwiches. Stock may be strengthened by adding beef bouillon cubes. Makes about 10 cups (2.25 L).

LEFTOVER BONE STOCK: Saved bones from steaks and roasts may be browned in 450°F (230°C) oven and then boiled with vegetables to make stock.

QUICK BEEF STOCK I: Use condensed beef broth or consommé, diluted as directed on can.

QUICK BEEF STOCK II: Dissolve beef bouillon cubes according to package directions. Use as recipe indicates.

Why is it children slam the doors in summer that they left open all winter.

Most everyone loves this flavor.

PEANUT BANANA SANDWICHES

Bread slices	8	8
Butter or margarine		
Smooth peanut butter		
Banana, sliced	2	2

Spread bread slices with butter. Cover with peanut butter. Arrange banana slices over top. If not serving right away, dip banana slices in lemon or orange juice. Top with bread slice. Cut before serving. Makes 4 sandwiches.

Variation: Jelly, jam or honey may be added.

PEANUT BACON SNACK: Spread bread or toast slice with smooth peanut butter. Spread a slice of crumbled bacon over top. Marmalade or jelly is optional.

PEANUT CRANBERRY SNACK: Butter 2 raisin bread slices. Spread 1 with cranberry sauce and the other with peanut butter. Top 1 slice with lettuce and cover with other slice.

PEANUT CARROT SPREAD

Smooth peanut butter	½ cup	125 mL
Shredded carrot	½ cup	125 mL
Mayonnaise	2 tbsp.	30 mL
Lemon juice	½ tsp.	2 mL

Stir together. Makes about 1 cup (250 mL). Peanut butter flavor is mild. Delicious on orange or date bread.

Pictured on page 71.

PEANUT RAISIN SPREAD

Smooth peanut butter	½ cup	125 mL
Chopped raisins	½ cup	125 mL
Chopped celery	½ cup	125 mL
Mayonnaise	2 - 3 tbsp.	30 - 50 mL

Stir together to mix, adding mayonnaise to taste as well as for moisture. Makes about 1½ cups (350 mL).

BEEF SLAW SANDWICHES

A sandwich and salad all in one.

Finely shredded cabbage	1 cup	250 mL
Finely shredded carrot	1/4 cup	50 mL
Commercial coleslaw dressing	1 tbsp.	15 mL
Prepared horseradish	1/2 tsp.	2 mL
Toast slices, buttered	8	8
Cheese slices	4	4
Sliced cooked roast beef		
Salt and pepper sprinkle		

Mix first 4 ingredients together. Set aside.

On 4 toast slices put cheese, layer of beef, and sprinkle with salt and pepper. Top with cabbage mixture. Cover with remaining toast slices. Makes 4.

Pictured on page 53.

BEEF ROLLS

Ground cooked roast beef	1 cup	250 mL
Grated Cheddar cheese	1/2 cup	125 mL
Mayonnaise	1/4 cup	50 mL
Salt	1/2 tsp.	2 mL
Pepper	1/8 tsp.	0.5 mL
Bread slices, buttered		

Mix first 5 ingredients together, adding more mayonnaise if too dry. Check seasoning.

Remove crusts from bread. Roll lightly with rolling pin. Spread with filling. Roll and secure with pick. Toast in 400°F (200°C) oven. Makes about 1 cup (250 mL) filling.

TANGY BEEF SPREAD

Ground cooked roast beef	2 cups	500 mL
Mayonnaise	1/4 cup	50 mL
Prepared horseradish	1 tsp.	5 mL
Milk or water	1/4 cup	50 mL
Salt	1/2 tsp.	2 mL

Mix together. Horseradish flavor is very mild. Makes about 2 cups (450 mL).

(continued on next page)

BEEF SALAD SPREAD

Ground cooked roast beef	2 cups	500 mL
Chopped celery	1 cup	250 mL
Chopped onion	2 tbsp.	30 mL
Sweet pickle relish	2 tbsp.	30 mL
Salt	1/2 tsp.	2 mL
Pepper	1/8 tsp.	0.5 mL
Mayonnaise	1/4 cup	60 mL
Lemon juice	1 tbsp.	15 mL

Mix all together. Excellent. Makes about 2½ cups (575 mL).

SUBMARINE

This popular item lends itself to creativity. Use beef, chicken, pro-cessed meats and even hot meat. Also called Po' Boy and Hero.

Submarine bun, split and buttered	1	1
Cheese slices, preferably white	2	2
Shredded lettuce to cover	1/4 cup	50 mL
Ham slices	2	2
Tomato slices to cover	4 - 6	4 - 6
Salt and pepper sprinkle		
Mayonnaise, mustard		

On bottom bun half, lay cheese slices that have been cut in half. Overlap somewhat. Spread lettuce over top, adding more as desired. Cut ham slices in half or use more and fold over. Put on top of lettuce, overlapping. Put tomato over ham. Sprinkle with salt and pepper. Spread top half of bun with mayonnaise and/or mustard. Place on top. Makes 1.

ONION RETREAT

Eating one of these onion sandwiches makes being alone worthwhile.

Bread slices, buttered	2	2
Large Spanish onion slice	1	1
Salt and pepper		

Between bread slices put onion. Sprinkle with salt and pepper. Makes 1 sandwich.

COTTAGE CHEESE SPREADS

Great ways to use this popular food and to add different flavors.

COTTAGE CARROT SPREAD

Cottage cheese, mashed	½ cup	125 mL
Shredded carrot	¼ cup	50 mL
Finely chopped nuts	2 tbsp.	30 mL
Mayonnaise	2 tbsp.	30 mL
Salt	¼ tsp.	1 mL

Mix all together. Makes about ⅔ cup (150 mL). Delicious.

COTTAGE DATE SPREAD

Cottage cheese, mashed	½ cup	125 mL
Ground dates	⅓ cup	75 mL
Finely chopped nuts	¼ cup	50 mL

Mix together. Makes about ¾ cup (150 mL). A slightly sweet flavor. Good.

COTTAGE PEPPER SPREAD

Cottage cheese	½ cup	125 mL
Chopped green onion	2 tbsp.	30 mL
Chopped green pepper	2 tbsp.	30 mL
Salt sprinkle		
Paprika sprinkle		

Combine all ingredients. Spread on toasted bun. Sprinkle with paprika. Makes about ½ cup (125 mL). Attractive looking spread.

1. Loaf O' Plenty page 109
2. Spud Special page 31

Pitcher and bowl from the Irma Trading Co. Ltd., operated from 1930 to 1947 by Edward and Ruby Elford, parents of Jean Paré.

A centerpiece that tastes as good as it looks.

French bread, unsliced	1	1
Butter, mayonnaise and mustard		
Mozzarella cheese slices	4	4
Swiss cheese slices	4	4
Ham slices	4	4
Salami slices	4	4
Pimiento loaf slices	4	4
Macaroni loaf slices	4	4
Red and green pepper rings	8	8
Lettuce		

Cut loaf to bottom but not through, into 16 slices. Spread with butter, mayonnaise and mustard in center to make 8 sandwiches.

Insert 1 cheese slice, 2 meat slices, 1 pepper slice and lettuce into each sandwich. Place on cutting board. Cut through bottom crust to serve. Makes 8.

Pictured on page 107.

MINI MUNCH: This offshoot provides 1 loaf per serving. Cut tiny loaf into 8 slices, leaving bottom intact. Butter as above. Insert salami pieces, hard-boiled egg slice, Swiss cheese, cut in quarters, and lettuce. Put this in a baggie with a twist tie for your best brown bagger yet.

Pictured on page 107.

LOBSTER SPREAD

By using this treat on open faced buns, a little goes a long way.

Lobster, cartilage removed	5 oz.	142 g
Hard-boiled eggs, chopped	2	2
Chopped celery	¼ cup	50 mL
Dry onion flakes, crushed	1 tsp.	5 mL
Mayonnaise	1 - 2 tbsp.	15 - 30 mL

Mix all together. Spread on buns. Makes about 1 cup (225 mL).

HAM SLAW HERO

Have your salad and meat on a bun. Sliced corned beef may also be used in these attractive meat rolls.

Finely shredded cabbage, packed	2 cups	500 mL
Finely chopped onion	¼ cup	50 mL
Vinegar	¼ cup	50 mL
Granulated sugar	⅓ cup	75 mL
Cooking oil	2 tbsp.	30 mL
Salt	½ tsp.	2 mL
Pepper	⅛ tsp.	0.5 mL
Cooked ham slices	6	6
Kaiser, onion or poppy seed rolls, split and buttered	2	2

Put cabbage and onion into bowl.

Heat next 5 ingredients in small saucepan until boiling. Pour over cabbage and onion. Press cabbage down. Let stand until cool. Chill.

To complete sandwich, drain cabbage well. Put a scant ¼ cup (50 mL) on each ham slice. Roll up jelly roll fashion. Place 3 rolls in each bun. Makes 2.

HAM SANDWICH: Layer ham, cheese (optional), lettuce, mayonnaise and mustard between 2 slices buttered bread.

HAM SWISS SNACK: Layer ham, Swiss cheese and tomato slices between 2 slices buttered rye bread. Lettuce, mustard and mayonnaise optional.

BEETROOT SANDWICH

Perhaps unusual but it's tasty.

Bread slices, buttered	2	2
Pickled beets, thinly sliced		
Marinated Onion Rings, page 11		

Cover 1 slice of bread with slices of beet. Add onion rings. Top with second bread slice. Cut and serve. Makes 1 serving.

Available year round, cucumbers make a light addition to any sand–wich.

CUCUMBER SANDWICH

Bread slices, buttered	2	2
Cucumber slices, peeled and sliced thinly	4 - 6	4 - 6
Salt and pepper sprinkle		
Alfalfa sprouts		
Mayonnaise (optional)		

Cover 1 slice of bread with cucumber slices. Sprinkle with salt and pepper. Lay sprouts over top. Spread second slice of bread with mayonnaise. Place over sprouts. Cut and serve. Makes 1 serving.

CUCUMBER HAM FILLING

Canned flaked ham	6½ oz.	184 g
Diced cucumber, peeled and seeded	2 cups	500 mL
Mayonnaise	½ cup	125 mL
Salt	½ tsp.	2 mL

Mix together. Makes about 2 cups (500 mL) of tasty filling.

CUCUMBER FILLING

Cream cheese	4 oz.	125 g
Finely diced cucumber, peeled and seeded	⅓ cup	75 mL
Sour cream	2 tbsp.	30 mL
Chopped chives	1 tsp.	5 mL
Salt and pepper sprinkle		

Mix together. Makes about ¾ cup (175 mL).

Worms didn't come off the ark in pairs. They came in apples.

SALMON FILLINGS

Red salmon gives the best color for sandwiches but pink has an equally good flavor.

SMOKED SALMON FILLING

Cream cheese, softened	4 oz.	125 g
Finely chopped onion	1 tbsp.	15 mL
Lemon juice	1 tsp.	5 mL
Prepared horseradish	1/2 tsp.	2 mL
Salt	1/8 tsp.	0.5 mL
Liquid smoke	1/2 tsp.	2 mL
Canned salmon, drained, skin and large bones removed	7 1/2 oz.	213 g

Mash first 6 ingredients together well.

Mix in salmon. Spread on croissant, crackers, or bread. Makes about 1 1/2 cups (350 mL). An expensive flavor for an ordinary price.

SALMON SPREAD

Canned salmon, drained, skin and large bones removed	7 1/2 oz.	213 g
Onion flakes, crushed	1/2 tsp.	2 mL
Parsley flakes	1/2 tsp.	2 mL
Salt	1/8 tsp.	0.5 mL
Mayonnaise	1/4 cup	50 mL

Mix well. Makes about 1 cup (250 mL). Quick and good.

SALMON EGG SPREAD

Canned salmon, drained, skin and large bones removed	7 1/2 oz.	213 g
Hard-boiled eggs, chopped	2	2
Chopped celery	1/4 cup	50 mL
Parsley flakes	1 tsp.	5 mL
Lemon juice	1 tsp.	5 mL
Salt	1/2 tsp.	2 mL
Mayonnaise	1/3 cup	75 mL

Combine all ingredients in bowl. Mix well. Makes about 1 1/2 cups (350 mL).

(continued on next page)

SALMON CROISSANT: Split and butter croissant. Cover with Salmon Spread. Add alfalfa sprouts.

Pictured on page 125.

SALMON CHEDDAR SPREAD

Canned salmon, drained, skin and large bones removed	7½ oz.	213 g
Grated Cheddar cheese	½ cup	125 mL
Chopped celery	¼ cup	50 mL
Onion flakes, crushed	2 tsp.	10 mL
Mayonnaise	2 tbsp.	30 mL

Mix all ingredients together. Check for salt and pepper. Makes about 1 cup (225 mL).

RIBBON SANDWICHES

Makes a moist sandwich using regular bread slices. An array of colors and flavors of your choice.

Brown bread slices, day old	4	4
White bread slices, day old	4	4
Butter or margarine, softened		
Fillings, different colors, such as ham, egg, salmon, beef, cheese, tuna	3	3

Use 2 white and 2 brown slices per stack. Use 3 different fillings, or only 1 filling, for each stack. Butter bread and spread fillings between slices, alternating brown and white bread. Wrap in plastic bag and chill. To serve, remove crusts and cut each stack into 3 or 4 strips. Makes 6 or 8 thick slices.

Pictured on page 35.

The main reason for so many divorces is matrimony.

PITA SANDWICHES

This fantastic pocket bread lends itself to cold or hot fillings.

Pita bread, cut in half and buttered inside	2	2
Shrimp Spread, page 118		
Shredded lettuce		
Cottage cheese	½ cup	125 mL
Chopped green pepper	2 tbsp.	30 mL
Avocado slices, cut small		
Lemon juice		
Alfalfa sprouts		
Whole shrimp (optional)		

Spread inside of pita bread with a thin layer of shrimp filling. Line with lettuce.

Mix cottage cheese with green pepper. Spoon into pita.

Dip avocado in lemon juice, then push partly into cottage cheese. Add a few sprouts. Arrange shrimp here and there. Makes 3 medium pita halves or 4 small.

Pictured on page 143.

PITA FILLINGS

Beef stroganoff, heated
Chili or pork and beans, heated
Sloppy Joe mixture, heated
Spaghetti with meat sauce, heated
Potato or macaroni salad, cold
Egg salad, cold
Tuna salad, cold

Bells are so easy to manage. They always sound off when tolled.

This New Orleans specialty is a combination of meat and cheese combined with an olive salad, all stuffed into a round loaf.

Chopped pimiento-stuffed olives	1 cup	250 mL
Chopped pimiento	¼ cup	50 mL
Chopped celery	½ cup	125 mL
Chopped green pepper	2 tbsp.	30 mL
Shredded carrot	2 tbsp.	30 mL
Garlic powder	¼ tsp.	1 mL
Ground oregano (optional)	¼ tsp.	1 mL
Olive oil or cooking oil	½ cup	125 mL
Red wine vinegar	½ cup	125 mL
Round Italian bread loaf, 10 inches (25 cm)	1	1
Genoa salami slices, to cover	4 - 6	4 - 6
Provolone cheese slices, to cover	4 - 6	4 - 6
Ham slices, to cover	4 - 6	4 - 6
Swiss cheese slices, to cover	4 - 6	4 - 6

Olive Salad: Mix first 9 ingredients together. Allow to marinate in refrigerator for several hours.

Slice loaf into 2 layers. Leaving about 1 inch (2.5 cm) around edges, remove bread from both layers about ½ inch (1 cm) deep. Brush layers with oil from olive salad.

Spoon drained olive mixture over bottom half. Layer remaining ingredients in order given. Cover with top half. Wrap in plastic or foil. Chill, with 2 or 3 pounds (1 or 1.5 kg) of butter or margarine used as a weight on top, for at least 20 to 30 minutes. Cut into wedges to serve. May also be served in Italian buns.

When ministers phone long distance, they talk parson to parson.

CREAM CHEESE SPREADS

CREAM OLIVE SPREAD

Cream cheese, softened	4 oz.	125 g
Chopped pimiento-stuffed olives	2 tbsp.	30 mL
Chopped celery	1 tsp.	5 mL
Chopped green pepper	1 tsp.	5 mL
Chopped green onion	1 tsp.	5 mL

Mix together. A good olive flavor. Makes about ½ cup (125 mL).

Pictured on page 71.

CREAM SWEET BUN: Spread bun half with cream cheese. Top with jelly, jam or marmalade. Broil.

CREAM PEPPER SPREAD

Cream cheese, softened	4 oz.	125 mL
Butter or margarine	¼ cup	50 mL
Chili sauce or ketchup	2 tbsp.	30 mL
Chopped green pepper	2 tbsp.	30 mL
Mayonnaise	2 tbsp.	30 mL

Mix all together. Makes about 1 cup (225 mL).

Pictured on page 71.

CREAM FRUIT SPREAD

Cream cheese, softened	4 oz.	125 g
Milk or cream	¼ cup	50 mL
Lemon juice	½ tsp.	2 mL
Chopped date	⅓ cup	75 mL
Chopped dried apricot	¼ cup	50 mL
Chopped raisins	¼ cup	50 mL
Chopped pecans or walnuts	¼ cup	50 mL

Thoroughly blend cheese, milk and lemon juice.

Add remaining ingredients. Delicious on raisin or nut bread. Makes about 1⅓ cups (300 mL).

(continued on next page)

CREAM ONION SPREAD

Cream cheese, softened	4 oz.	125 g
Chopped chive	2 tbsp.	30 mL
Milk or cream	1 tsp.	5 mL
Salt and pepper sprinkle		

Mash together. Makes about ½ cup (125 mL). Good onion flavor.

CREAM BLUE SPREAD

Cream cheese, softened	4 oz.	125 g
Crumbled blue cheese	2 tbsp.	30 mL
Mayonnaise	⅓ cup	75 mL
Finely chopped walnuts	½ cup	125 mL
Worcestershire sauce	½ tsp.	2 mL
Onion salt	⅛ tsp.	0.5 mL

Mix all together well. Makes about 1 cup (250 mL). Blue cheese flavor is quite mild. An excellent spread.

AVOCADO FILLINGS

Avocado has made its way into sandwiches to the delight of many.

AVOCADO FILLING

Avocado, peeled	1	1
Onion flakes, crushed	1 tsp.	5 mL
Lemon juice	1 tbsp.	15 mL
Salt and pepper sprinkle		

Mash all together. Makes about ¼ cup (60 mL).

AVOCADO CHEESE FILLING

Avocado, peeled	1	1
Cream cheese	8 oz.	250 g
Mayonnaise	¼ cup	50 mL
Lemon juice	1 tbsp.	15 mL

Mash together well. Makes about 1½ cups (350 mL) of creamy light green filling.

SHRIMP AND CRAB FILLINGS

It is so easy to keep ingredients on hand for these fillings.

SHRIMP CREAM SPREAD

Canned shrimp, rinsed and drained	4 oz.	113 g
Cream cheese, softened	4 oz.	125 g
Chili sauce	1 tsp.	5 mL
Lemon juice	1/2 tsp.	2 mL
Worcestershire sauce	1/2 tsp.	2 mL
Small pinch garlic powder	1	1
Mayonnaise	2 tbsp.	30 mL
Dry dill weed	1/8 tsp.	0.5 mL

Mash together. Makes about 1 cup (250 mL).

SHRIMP SPREAD

Canned broken shrimp, rinsed and drained	4 oz.	113 g
Butter or margarine, softened	1/4 cup	50 mL
Mayonnaise	1/4 cup	50 mL
Lemon juice	1 1/2 tsp.	7 mL
Parsley flakes	1 tsp.	5 mL
Onion powder	1/4 tsp.	1 mL

Mash together. Makes a generous 1 cup (250 mL).

SHRIMP EGG SPREAD

Canned broken shrimp, rinsed and drained	4 oz.	113 g
Hard-boiled eggs, chopped	2	2
Finely chopped celery	1/4 cup	50 mL
Mayonnaise	2 tbsp.	30 mL
Lemon juice	1 tsp.	5 mL
Onion powder	1/4 tsp.	1 mL
Salt	1/4 tsp.	1 mL

Mash together. Makes about 1 1/2 cups (350 mL).

(continued on next page)

CRAB SPREAD

Canned crab, drained and cartilage removed	5 oz.	142 g
Cream cheese, softened	4 oz.	125 g
Lemon juice	1 tsp.	5 mL
Dry dill weed	1/8 - 1/4 tsp.	0.5 - 1 mL

Mash together, adding dill weed to taste. Makes about 1 cup (225 mL).

SANDWICH LOAF

A gorgeous ribbon loaf frosted with cream cheese. Serve with a fork.

White sandwich loaf, day old, unsliced (or use brown and white)	1	1
Butter or margarine, softened	1/2 cup	125 mL
Different sandwich fillings, about 1 cup (250 mL) each such as egg, ham and salmon	3	3
Cream cheese, softened	12 oz.	375 g
Milk	3 - 4 tbsp.	45 - 60 mL
Snipped parsley and/or chopped nuts		

Cut crusts from bread. Slice bread lengthwise into 4 thick slices. Lay 1 slice on platter or tray. Butter and spread with 1 filling. Butter second slice on 1 side. Place buttered side down on filling. Butter and spread with second filling. Repeat. Butter only 1 side of top slice and place buttered side down. Wrap firmly in plastic or foil. Chill at least 1 hour.

Frosting: Beat cream cheese, milk and sugar until of good spreading consistency. Frost loaf. Decorate with parsley and/or nuts. Chill. To serve, cut into thick slices.

Pare Pointer

A boy who takes a bath without being told is probably giving the dog one.

TUNA FILLINGS

It is hard to beat taste combined with economy.

TUNA CHEESE FILLING

Canned tuna, drained	6½ oz.	184 g
Cream cheese, softened	4 oz.	125 g
Butter or margarine	¼ cup	50 mL
Finely chopped onion	½ cup	125 mL
Lemon juice	1 tsp.	5 mL
Salt	⅛ tsp.	0.5 mL
Pepper	⅛ tsp.	0.5 mL
Ground nuts (optional)	½ cup	125 mL

Mash together well. Makes a scant 2 cups (450 mL). Very tasty.

TUNA CHEDDAR SPREAD

Canned tuna, drained	6½ oz.	184 g
Grated Cheddar cheese	1 cup	250 mL
Finely chopped onion	2 tbsp.	30 mL
Sweet pickle relish	2 tbsp.	30 mL
Hard-boiled eggs, chopped	2	2
Salt	½ tsp.	2 mL
Mayonnaise	⅓ cup	75 mL

Stir together well to mix. Add a bit more mayonnaise if needed for taste and for moisture. Makes about 2 cups (450 mL).

TUNA BUNS: Cover 6 bun halves with Tuna Cheddar Spread. Wrap in foil. Heat in 350°F (180°C) oven until hot, about 20 minutes.

ZIPPY TUNA SPREAD

Canned tuna, drained	6½ oz.	184 g
Mayonnaise	¼ cup	50 mL
Prepared horseradish (mild)	2 tsp.	10 mL
Lemon juice	1 tsp.	5 mL
Salt	½ tsp.	2 mL
Pepper	⅛ tsp.	0.5 mL

Mix together well. Spread on buns and broil. Top with a cheese slice first if desired. Makes about ¾ cup (175 mL).

(continued on next page)

TUNA PINEAPPLE SPREAD

Canned tuna, drained	6½ oz.	184 g
Finely chopped celery	¼ cup	50 mL
Crushed pineapple, drained	¼ cup	50 mL
Chopped walnuts	2 tbsp.	30 mL
Mayonnaise	¼ cup	50 mL

Stir together. Check to see if salt is needed. Makes about 1⅓ cups (300 mL).

TUNA FILLING

Canned tuna, drained	6½ oz.	184 g
Finely chopped celery	¼ cup	50 mL
Onion flakes, crushed	1 tsp.	5 mL
Salt	⅛ tsp.	0.5 mL
Mayonnaise	¼ cup	50 mL

Mix all together. The easiest ever. Makes about ⅔ cup (150 mL).

MOZZARELLA SANDWICH

Another great standby.

Mozzarella cheese slice	1	1
Tomato slices to cover	2 - 3	2 - 3
Salt and pepper sprinkle		
Light sprinkle sweet basil		
Slice of ham	1	1
Lettuce to cover		
Bread slices	2	2

Layer first 6 ingredients between bread slices. Butter outside. Grill. Makes 1.

A bird that sits all the time is better known as a stool pigeon.

HAM FILLINGS

Another all time favorite meat filling.

HAM AND CHEDDAR FILLING

Canned flaked ham	6½ oz.	184 g
Grated Cheddar cheese	¾ cup	175 mL
Sweet pickle relish	2 tbsp.	30 mL
Finely chopped onion	1 tbsp.	15 mL
Mayonnaise	2 tbsp.	30 mL
Prepared mustard	1 tsp.	5 mL

Mix together. Fill buns. Wrap in foil. Heat in 350°F (180°C) oven until hot, about 20 minutes. May also be spread on bun halves and broiled. Makes about 1½ cups (350 mL).

HAM SPREAD

Canned flaked ham	6½ oz.	184 g
Sweet pickle relish	1 tbsp.	15 mL
Onion flakes, crushed	½ tsp.	2 mL
Mayonnaise	4 tsp.	20 mL

Mash all together, adding a bit more mayonnaise if too dry. Makes enough for 4 sandwiches.

CANNED MEAT FILLING: Use canned meat such as Prem, Kam, Spam, Klik instead of ham. Double remaining ingredients.

NUTTY CHEESE SPREAD

Ever popular Cheddar served with a crunch.

Grated Cheddar cheese	1 cup	250 mL
Chopped walnuts	⅔ cup	150 mL
Parsley flakes	2 tsp.	10 mL
Onion flakes, crushed	2 tsp.	10 mL
Mayonnaise	½ cup	125 mL

Mix all ingredients together. Makes about 1 cup (250 mL). Tasty and nutty.

Pictured on cover.

A very popular sandwich, always in demand.

EGG FILLING

Hard-boiled eggs, chopped	6	6
Finely diced celery	3 tbsp.	50 mL
Salt	1/2 tsp.	2 mL
Parsley flakes	1/2 tsp.	2 mL
Onion powder	1/4 tsp.	1 mL
Mayonnaise	1/4 cup	50 mL

Mix all together. Makes about 1½ cups (350 mL). Spreads easily.

EGG SALAD SPREAD

Hard-boiled eggs, chopped	6	6
Diced cucumber, peeled and seeded	1 cup	250 mL
Diced celery	1 cup	250 mL
Chopped green onion	3 tbsp.	50 mL
Chopped pimiento	2 tbsp.	30 mL
Salt	1 tsp.	5 mL
Mayonnaise	1/2 cup	125 mL

Mix all together being sure to drain diced cucumber well. Makes about 3 cups (700 mL).

EGG CHEESE SPREAD

Hard-boiled eggs, cut up	4	4
Cheddar cheese, cubed	1 cup	250 mL
Small onion, cut up	1	1
Salt	1/2 tsp.	2 mL
Pepper	1/4 tsp.	1 mL

Grind all ingredients. If needed, add some melted butter or margarine to moisten. Makes about 2⅓ cups (525 mL).

Barking dogs should always be fed hush puppies.

CLUBHOUSE

You can never go wrong with this, whether you serve it for lunch or an evening after-the-game snack.

Toast slices, buttered	3	3
Turkey slice to fit	1	1
Salt and pepper sprinkle		
Lettuce to cover		
Mayonnaise to cover		
Tomato slices to cover	2 - 3	2 - 3
Salt and pepper sprinkle		
Bacon slices, crispy-fried	2 - 3	2 - 3

Layer first slice of toast with turkey, salt and pepper sprinkle, lettuce and mayonnaise. Top with second slice of toast.

Layer second slice of toast with tomatoes. Sprinkle with salt and pepper. Cut bacon slices in half and arrange over tomato. Top with remaining toast. Pierce each quarter with a pick. Cut diagonally into 4 sections. A thin pickle may be speared on top of each. Makes 1 serving.

JUMBO CLUBO: Make 1 layer turkey or chicken, lettuce and ham, the other layer tomato, bacon and cheese.

JUNIOR CLUB: Use only 2 slices toast. Layer with mayonnaise, lettuce, chicken, tomato and bacon.

1. Tomato Rice Soup page 74
2. Chicken Noodle Soup page 74
3. Lettuce Soup page 32
4. Salmon Croissant page 113
5. Asparagus Ham Roll page 146
6. Bun Scramble page 134

CORNED BEEF SPREAD

With ingredients on hand, this seldom-thought-of meat works won–ders.

Canned corned beef, mashed	12 oz.	340 g
Hard-boiled eggs, chopped	2	2
Mayonnaise	¹/₂ cup	125 mL
Onion flakes	2 tsp.	10 mL
Water	2 tsp.	10 mL
Worcestershire sauce	1 tsp.	5 mL

Mix corned beef and eggs in bowl.

In small bowl combine next 4 ingredients. Stir and add to corned beef mixture. Mix together. Spread on rye bread, pumpernickel or crackers. Makes about 2¹/₂ cups (600 mL).

Pictured on cover.

OLIVE NUT FILLING

This is for olive lovers.

Chopped walnuts	¹/₂ cup	125 mL
Shredded lettuce	¹/₂ cup	125 mL
Chopped pimiento-stuffed olives	¹/₂ cup	125 mL
Mayonnaise	¹/₄ cup	60 mL

Stir all together. Has delicious flavor. Makes about 1 cup (250 mL).

Pare Pointer

Lipstick on a man shows he's been kissed. Lipstick on a woman shows she hasn't.

CHICKEN SUBMARINE

Roast a large enough chicken to have lots left over for sandwiches or roast some for sandwiches alone.

Submarine roll, split and buttered	1	1
Spinach leaves or Romaine lettuce	4 - 6	4 - 6
Sliced chicken to cover		
Salt and pepper sprinkle		
Provolone or Swiss cheese slice	1	1
Salami slices	4	4
Green pepper rings	4	4
Mayonnaise or Italian dressing		

Layer on bottom of bun all ingredients in order given. This makes a neater job if bottom is hollowed out a bit first. Add bun top. Make a single for each serving or make up a large loaf to be cut as needed.

CHICKEN HAM SANDWICH: Butter 2 slices bread. Cover 1 slice with cranberry sauce, sliced chicken, salt and pepper sprinkle and a slice of ham. Lettuce is optional. Serve as is or butter outside and grill.

CHICKEN CHEESE GRILL: Layer sliced chicken and cheese slice between 2 slices buttered bread. Spread outside with a mixture of 1 tbsp. (15 mL) butter or margarine and 1/16 tsp. (0.5 mL) poultry seasoning. Grill.

CHICKEN ASPARAGUS SANDWICH: Layer cheese slice, sliced chicken, salt and pepper sprinkle and 4 cooked asparagus spears between 2 buttered bread slices.

CHICKEN SALAD SPREAD

Ground cooked chicken	2 cups	500 mL
Chopped celery	1/2 cup	125 mL
Salt	3/4 tsp.	3 mL
Lemon juice	1 tsp.	5 mL
Mayonnaise	1/2 cup	125 mL
Parsley flakes	1 tsp.	5 mL
Onion powder	1/4 tsp.	1 mL

Mix all together. Check for seasoning. Makes about 1½ cups (350 mL).

(continued on next page)

CHICKEN ALMOND SPREAD

Ground cooked chicken	2 cups	500 mL
Toasted ground almonds - toast in 350°F (180°C) oven for 10 to 15 minutes	¾ cup	175 mL
Mayonnaise	½ cup	125 mL
Parsley flakes	1 tsp.	5 mL
Seasoned salt	1 tsp.	5 mL

Mix together well, adding up to ¼ cup (50 mL) more mayonnaise to taste. Milk may be added if too dry. A good nutty spread. Makes about 1½ cups (350 mL).

CHICKEN CURRY SPREAD: Add about ½ tsp. (2 mL) curry powder to Chicken Almond Spread.

TACO DOGS

A great twist to a great snack.

Taco shell	1	1
Wiener, halved lengthwise and fried	1	1
Chili con carne, heated	2 tbsp.	30 mL
Grated Monterey Jack cheese	1 tbsp.	15 mL
Shredded lettuce	2 tbsp.	30 mL
Diced tomato	1 tbsp.	15 mL
Grated Cheddar cheese (optional)	1 tbsp.	15 mL

In taco shell, put hot fried wiener. Add chili and put Jack cheese on top. Heat in 350°F (180°C) oven to melt cheese.

Layer lettuce, tomato and Cheddar cheese over top. Makes 1.

Vampires are a pain in the neck.

BEEF BROIL

Have hamburger mixture chilled and ready to assemble. To spread and broil takes very little time.

Ground beef	1 lb.	450 g
Small onion, finely chopped	1	1
Salt	1 tsp.	5 mL
Pepper	1/4 tsp.	1 mL
Hamburger buns, halved	4	4

Mix first 4 ingredients together.

Toast uncut sides of 8 bun halves under broiler. Turn. Spread meat mixture on cut, untoasted sides right to edges. Broil 3 to 4 inches (7 to 10 cm) from heat to cook, about 15 minutes. Makes 8.

TUNA PUFFS

A golden puff with tomato hidden.

Canned tuna, drained	6 1/2 oz.	184 g
Finely chopped celery	1/4 cup	50 mL
Onion powder	1/8 tsp.	0.5 mL
Salt	1/8 tsp.	0.5 mL
Mayonnaise	1/4 cup	50 mL
Hamburger buns, split and buttered	3	3
Tomato slices	6	6
Mayonnaise	1/2 cup	125 mL
Grated Cheddar cheese	1/4 cup	60 mL

Mix first 5 ingredients together.

Spread on bun halves.

Top with tomato slice.

Combine mayonnaise with cheese. Spread over all. Broil about 4 inches (10 cm) from heat. Makes 6.

Pictured on page 143.

These make a good change from hamburgers, especially if you catch your own fish.

Fish fillets	1 lb.	454 g
All-purpose flour to coat		
Pancake mix	1 cup	250 mL
Club soda	1 cup	250 mL
Fat for deep-frying		
Tartar sauce or mayonnaise, and		
lettuce for garnish		
Hamburger buns, split and buttered	4 - 6	4 - 6

Cut fish fillets to fit buns. Coat well with flour. Allow to dry for 10 to 15 minutes.

Stir pancake mix and club soda together well, adding more liquid if needed. Dip fish pieces in batter.

Carefully drop into hot fat, 400°F (200°C), to cook and brown. Drain on paper towel.

Serve in bun with tartar sauce or mayonnaise. Lettuce may be added as well. Makes 4 to 6 servings.

In about fifty years movies went from being silent to unspeakable.

CORNED HERO

Gooey to eat but makes an impressive sight. Make one large loaf or 2 smaller ones.

French bread loaf	1	1
Sour cream	¼ cup	50 mL
Mayonnaise	2 tbsp.	30 mL
Chopped chives	1 tsp.	5 mL
Parsley flakes	1 tsp.	5 mL
Onion powder	⅛ tsp.	0.5 mL

Tomato slices to cover
Corned beef slices to cover
Cheese slices to cover

Slice bread in half horizontally. Toast in hot oven or under broiler. Butter each half.

Mix next 5 ingredients together. Spread on flat side of bottom loaf half.

Layer with tomato slices, corned beef and cheese. Broil to melt and slightly brown cheese. Cover with bread top. Cuts into 4 sections.

Note: If you prefer a thinner loaf, cut out a horizontal center slice and use for another purpose.

Pictured on page 89.

If you want to clear people out of the way, just blow your own horn.

Served in style.

Butter or margarine	1 tbsp.	15 mL
Medium onion, chopped	1	1
Ground beef	1 lb.	450 g
Canned tomato paste	5½ oz.	156 mL
Water	1 cup	225 mL
Chili powder	2 tsp.	10 mL
Salt	1 tsp.	5 mL
Pepper	¼ tsp.	1 mL
Submarine buns	6	6

Put butter, onion and ground beef into frying pan. Scramble-fry until meat is cooked.

Add next 5 ingredients. Simmer 5 minutes.

Cut thin layer from top of bun which can be used as a lid. Hollow out bun. Fill with about ½ cup (125 mL) filling. Use bun lid if desired. Makes about 3 cups (675 mL).

Pictured on page 89.

Whether in toasted bread rolls or heated on buns, this is a winner every time.

Cream cheese, softened	4 oz.	125 g
Canned crab, cartilage removed	5 oz.	142 g
Finely chopped onion	1 tbsp.	15 mL
Prepared horseradish	¼ tsp.	1 mL
Salt	⅛ tsp.	0.5 mL
Ground almonds	2 tbsp.	30 mL

Bread slices, crust removed

Mash first 6 ingredients together. Spread on bread slices that have been rolled lightly to prevent breaking. Roll and secure with picks. May use as is but very good when toasted in 400°F (200°C) oven. Makes about 1½ cups (350 mL) of filling.

BUN SCRAMBLE

A cross between a Denver and Benedict Bun. A hearty snack.

Finely chopped onion	1 tbsp.	15 mL
Butter or margarine	1 tsp.	5 mL
Egg	1	1
Water	1 tbsp.	15 mL
English muffin, split, toasted and buttered - or hot dog bun	1	1
Ham slice or crispy bacon	1	1
Tomato slice	1	1
Shredded lettuce	2 tbsp.	30 mL

Sauté onion in butter until clear and soft.

Add egg and water. Scramble-fry.

On bottom half of toasted muffin, layer ham, tomato and lettuce. Top with scrambled egg mixture. Cover with muffin top. Makes 1.

Pictured on page 125.

DENVER SANDWICH

You will find this gratifying any time of day. Also called Western. Double quantity for a thick sandwich.

Egg	1	1
Water or milk	1 tbsp.	15 mL
Chopped ham	2 tbsp.	30 mL
Finely chopped onion	1 tbsp.	15 mL
Finely chopped green pepper	1 tbsp.	15 mL
Salt sprinkle		
Pepper sprinkle		
Toast slices, buttered	2	2

With spoon, beat egg and water together in bowl. Add ham, onion, green pepper, salt and pepper. Pour slowly into hot, well greased frying pan. It will start to cook and won't spread too much. As it cooks, keep drawing to center to keep bread-shape. Brown lightly. Turn to brown other side.

Put between toast slices. Cut and serve hot. Makes 1 serving.

Bologna lovers — you are in for a treat.

Hamburger bun, halved and buttered	1	1
Bologna slices	2	2
Salami slices	2 - 4	2 - 4
Sauerkraut, rinsed and drained	¹/₂ cup	125 mL
Grated Mozzarella cheese	¹/₂ cup	125 mL

On each bun half, layer ingredients in order given. Broil. Meat will curl upward forming a cup. Makes 2.

Pictured on page 53.

BOLOGNA FILLING

Ground bologna	¹/₂ cup	125 mL
Hard-boiled egg, chopped	1	1
Pickle relish	2 tbsp.	30 mL
Onion flakes	1 tsp.	5 mL
Mayonnaise	2 tbsp.	30 mL
Salt	¹/₄ tsp.	1 mL

Mix together. Makes about ²/₃ cup (150 mL). Tasty.

MONTE CRISTO

A sandwich of popular fillings, dipped in egg and grilled.

White bread slices, buttered	3	3
Mozzarella cheese slices	2	2
Cooked ham slice	1	1
Sliced turkey or chicken	1	1
Egg, lightly beaten	1	1
Water	2 tbsp.	30 mL

Layer first bread slice with a slice of cheese, then ham. Top with second bread slice. Put turkey, then remaining cheese on top. Cover with third bread slice.

Mix egg with water. Dip sandwich into egg mixture. Grill in well greased frying pan, browning both sides. Cut diagonally into 4. Makes 1 large serving.

CHEESE WITH BACON BUNS

An old favorite sure to be a hit every time.

Hamburger buns	6	6
Processed cheese spread		
Thin bacon slices, cut in ½ inch (1 cm) pieces	6	6

Cut hamburger buns in half. Spread each half with cheese and place on baking sheet. Lay bacon pieces here and there over buns. Partially cook bacon if you want it to be crisp when finished. Broil until bacon sizzles. Makes 12 halves.

Note: To make these extra fast, spread buns with cheese, sprinkle with bacon bits and broil.

BACON CHEESE ROLL UPS: Roll crustless bread slice lightly with rolling pin. Spread with processed cheese. Lay 4 half slices of cooked bacon on top. Roll. Secure with picks. Brush with melted butter or margarine. Toast in 400°F (200°C) oven or broil.

CHEESE ROLL UPS: Use processed cheese spread only in roll.

JAM ROLL UPS: Spread crustless bread slice with butter or margarine. Spread with mixture of jelly, jam or honey. Roll. Secure with picks. Toast in 400°F (200°C) oven. A real treat.

SEAFOOD BAKE

These can be kept chilled, then toasted in the oven just before lunch. Filling may be used on buns or in sandwiches.

Canned tuna, drained	6½ oz.	184 g
Canned broken shrimp, drained	4 oz.	113 g
Finely chopped celery	½ cup	125 mL
Salt	¼ tsp.	1 mL
Pepper	⅛ tsp.	0.5 mL
Mayonnaise	⅓ cup	75 mL
Grated Cheddar cheese	1 cup	250 mL
Marinated Onion Rings, page 11		

(continued on next page)

Mix first 6 ingredients together. Spread on bun halves or bread. Add some cheese and onion rings. Add second slice of bread. Brush with melted butter or margarine. Place on baking sheet. Toast in 400°F (200°C) oven for about 10 minutes. Makes 2 cups (450 mL) of filling.

TUNA HERO: Spread hero roll with your favorite tuna filling. Add layers of sliced tomato, cheese, lettuce and mayonnaise. Marinated onion rings are a good addition. Eat as is or broil.

FRANKLY CHEESE BUNS

A boon to the cook to have a different way to serve frankfurters.

Grated Cheddar cheese	1 cup	250 mL
Milk	3 tbsp.	50 mL
Prepared mustard	1 tbsp.	15 mL
Wieners, chopped	3	3
Hot dog buns, uncut	3	3

Heat cheese, milk and mustard in double boiler or heavy saucepan, stirring often, until cheese melts.

Add wieners. Stir to heat through.

Cut a V shaped wedge from each bun. Spoon hot wiener mixture into cavity. Makes 3.

Pictured on page 53.

HOT DOG SUPREME: Spread split bun with processed cheese. Insert 1 wiener and 2 bacon slices, half cooked. Broil 5 inches (12.5 cm) from heat until sizzling hot. Makes 1.

Pare Pointer

It is a cool politician who accuses his opponent of fooling the public, yet manages to keep the envy out of his voice.

SPECIAL GRILLED CHEESE

An old standby with sliced onions. Unless you try them you won't know how well onions go with cheese. Foolproof variations for kids of all ages.

Bread slices, buttered	2	2
Cheese slice	1	1
Thinly sliced onion (or use Marinated Onion Rings, page 11)	2 tbsp.	30 mL

Place one slice of bread, buttered side down in hot frying pan. Put cheese slice on top. Arrange onion over. Top with remaining bread slice, buttered side up. Brown well, turn and brown second side. Cut and serve hot. Makes 1 serving.

OPEN CHEESE SUBS: On buttered submarine bun halves, lay cheese triangles, overlapping slightly. Top with onion rings. Sprinkle with paprika. Broil.

HAM AND CHEESE SANDWICH: Insert slices of ham and cheese between 2 slices of buttered bread or toast. Add lettuce along with mayonnaise and/or mustard. May also be grilled.

CHEESE AND TOMATO SANDWICH: Layer cheese, sliced tomato and lettuce between buttered bread or toast. Add mayonnaise. Salt and pepper as desired.

TOMATO AND LETTUCE SANDWICH: Put sliced tomatoes, topped with lettuce between buttered bread or toast. Add mayonnaise, or commercial sandwich spread, salt and pepper as desired.

A tough chick comes from a hard-boiled egg.

Cutting these in half exposes a colorful layer of asparagus, cheese and tomato.

Toast slices, buttered	2	2
Tomato slices	4 - 6	4 - 6
Cheese slices	2	2
Asparagus spears, canned or fresh (cooked)	8	8
Egg white	1	1
Egg yolk	1	1
French dressing	1 tsp.	5 mL
Salt and pepper sprinkle	1	1

On 2 slices toast, layer tomato, cheese and asparagus.

Beat egg white until stiff.

Mix egg yolk, dressing, salt and pepper together. Fold into egg white. Spread over asparagus. Bake in 350°F (180°C) oven until light brown, about 15 minutes. Cut in half to serve. Makes 2.

Pictured on page 53.

PARMESAN PUFFS

Grated Parmesan cheese	½ cup	125 mL
Mayonnaise	2 tbsp.	30 mL
Finely chopped onion	6 tbsp.	100 mL
Butter or margarine, softened	1 tbsp.	15 mL

Mix together. Use as a spread for toast which is then broiled. Makes about ½ cup (125 mL).

She may be good at mending bowls but she has been around cracked pots too long.

REUBEN SANDWICH

Served hot, this is a people-favorite.

Rye bread slices or pumpernickel	2	2
Thin slices corned beef	2 - 4	2 - 4
Sauerkraut, rinsed and drained	2 tbsp.	30 mL
Mozzarella cheese slice	1	1

On 1 slice bread layer corned beef, sauerkraut and cheese. Cover with second slice bread. Butter outside of sandwich. Grill. Makes 1 sand-wich.

Variation: Spread 1 slice bread with Thousand Island salad dressing before adding filling.

BACON REUBEN: Use Canadian bacon, fried, in place of corned beef.

SLAW REUBEN: Use coleslaw instead of sauerkraut.

REUBEN BURGER: Cook hamburger patty. Top with slice of Mozzarella or Swiss cheese, then a scoop of sauerkraut. Continue cooking until cheese melts. Transfer to buttered hamburger bun, preferably toasted.

CORNED BEEF SANDWICH: Layer lots of thinly sliced corned beef between 2 slices of buttered rye or pumpernickel bread. Mix ½ tsp. (2 mL) prepared mustard with ¼ tsp. (1 mL) prepared horseradish and spread on. Add lettuce and you have a real sandwich.

Astronauts can't land on the moon when it's full.

Kids of all ages choose these first. So easy.

Butter or margarine	1 tbsp.	15 mL
Lean ground beef	1 lb.	500 g
Chopped onion	½ cup	125 mL
Salt	1 tsp.	5 mL
Canned tomato paste	5½ oz.	156 mL
Worcestershire sauce	1 tsp.	5 mL
Italian seasoning	1 tsp.	5 mL
English muffins, split and buttered	6	6
Mozzarella cheese slices	6	6
Grated Parmesan cheese	2 tbsp.	30 mL
Chopped green onion	¼ cup	50 mL

Melt butter in frying pan. Add ground beef, onion and salt. Fry slowly until cooked.

Add tomato paste, Worcestershire sauce and Italian seasoning. Stir.

Spread over muffin halves. Cut cheese slices in half. Put ½ slice on each bun half. Sprinkle with Parmesan cheese. Top with onion. Broil. Makes 12.

CORNED BEEF BUNS

Spoon this cheesy spread on buns and bake for a delicious snack.

Mild processed cheese, cut up (Velveeta is good)	4 oz.	125 g
Butter or margarine	2 tbsp.	30 mL
Prepared mustard	1 tsp.	5 mL
Onion powder	¼ tsp.	1 mL
Canned corned beef, chopped	12 oz.	340 g

Put cheese, butter, mustard and onion powder into saucepan. Heat over low heat, stirring frequently, until melted.

Add corned beef. Stir. Spread on split buns. Bake in 400°F (200°C) oven for 10 to 15 minutes. Makes about 1½ cups (350 mL).

MUSHROOM TRIANGLES

Try this filling on open faced buns, broiled, as well as in these tasty triangles.

Sliced fresh mushrooms - ¼ lb. (113 g)	1½ cups	350 mL
Chopped onion	¼ cup	50 mL
Butter or margarine	1 tbsp.	15 mL
Cream cheese, cut up	4 oz.	125 g
Worcestershire sauce	¼ tsp.	1 mL
Salt	¼ tsp.	1 mL
Pepper sprinkle		
Garlic powder sprinkle		

Sauté mushrooms and onion in butter until onion is clear and soft.

Add remaining ingredients. Stir to melt cheese. Spread on buttered crustless bread. Fold to make triangle. Press edges. May also be spread on crustless bread slices. Roll and secure with picks. Brush with melted butter or margarine. Toast triangles or rolls in 400°F (200°C) oven for about 10 to 15 minutes. Makes about ⅔ cup (150 mL).

SIMPLE MUSHROOM ROLLS: Roll crustless bread lightly with rolling pin. Spread with condensed cream of mushroom soup. Roll and secure with picks. Brush with melted butter or margarine. Toast in 400°F (200°C) oven or brush with melted butter and broil.

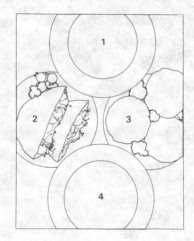

1. Lobster Chowder page 93
2. Pita Sandwiches page 114
3. Tuna Puffs page 130
4. Neptune Chowder page 95

You will find it difficult to wait until this is cool enough to slice.

Loaf of frozen bread	1	1
Provolone cheese, thin slices	6	6
Cooked ham, thin slices	6	6
Mozzarella cheese slices	6	6
Grated Parmesan cheese	2 - 4 tbsp.	30 - 50 mL

Allow bread to thaw and double in size. Work down. Roll into rec–tangular shape as thinly as you can, ¼ inch (1 cm) or less. Have 1 side measure about 12 inches (30 cm).

Cut Provolone and Mozzarella cheese and ham into 4 strips per slice. This will allow for better expansion of dough. Arrange Provolone from edge of short side of dough, leaving long sides uncovered 1½ inches (3.5 cm) in from edge, also leaving at least 2 inches (5 cm) uncovered at other short end. Repeat with ham and Mozzarella. Sprinkle with Parmesan. Now dampen all edges, except short side where cheese and ham are at edge. Roll from that edge. Press to seal. Squeeze ends together. Place in a greased 9 × 5 inch (23 × 12 cm) pan seam side down. Brush with egg if desired. Cover with waxed paper. Place tea towel over all. Allow to rise until double in size. Remove towel and waxed paper. Bake in 400°F (200°C) oven for about 25 minutes until dark brown. Cool for about 30 minutes. Cut into 8 slices.

The story about the peacock is a beautiful tale.

ASPARAGUS HAM ROLLS

Hot toasted rolls make a different lunch treat, especially when they can be made ahead and chilled until needed.

Bread slices, crust removed	12	12
Butter or margarine		
Cooked ham slices	12	12
Asparagus spears, canned or fresh (cooked)	12	12
Cheese slices (optional)		

Roll bread slices lightly with rolling pin. Spread with butter. Add slice of ham. Put asparagus spear on one side. Roll and secure with toothpick. May be covered with damp tea towel to hold in refrigerator. To serve, place on baking sheet. Brown in 400°F (200°C) oven about 10 minutes. These brown better if brushed with melted butter or margarine first. Makes 12.

Pictured on page 125.

Variation: Use asparagus and cheese only, or ham and a bit of mustard.

LASAGNE SANDWICH

This is grilled and is indeed reminiscent of lasagne.

Bread slices	2	2
Mozzarella cheese slice	1	1
Sour cream	1 tbsp.	15 mL
Dry onion flakes, crushed	1 tsp.	5 mL
Oregano	1/8 tsp.	0.5 mL
Tomato slices to cover	2 - 3	2 - 3
Bacon slices, cooked, halved	2 - 3	2 - 3

On 1 slice bread put cheese.

Mix sour cream, onion and oregano together. Spread over cheese slice.

Arrange tomato slices over sour cream mixture. Put bacon over top and cover with second bread slice. Butter outside and grill. Makes 1.

Makes a good barbecue feast.

Hamburger bun, split and buttered	1	1
Ketchup, mustard or horseradish for garnish		
Sirloin steak, fairly thin and bun size, fried or broiled	1	1
Tomato slice for garnish		
Lettuce for garnish		

Spread bun with ketchup, mustard or horseradish. Add steak. Tomato and lettuce can be served in bun or on the side. Makes 1.

BEEF ON A BUN: Cook roast beef, about same size in diameter as bun, to desired doneness. Stack several thin, hot slices into buttered bun. Pass mustard, horseradish and ketchup.

BEEF DIP: Put 5 lbs. (2.2 kg) boneless beef roast such as a sirloin tip into roasting pan. Add water to come halfway up sides of meat. Cover and roast in 275°F (140°C) oven for about 4 hours. A chuck or blade roast may need to be roasted a bit longer until tender. Remove meat. Strain juice and measure. Dissolve 3 or 4 beef bouillon cubes - ⅕ oz. (6 g) size - in 6 cups (1.3 L) juice. Add 1 tsp. (5 mL) salt, or to taste. Use proportionally less salt if juice volume is less. Celery salt, onion powder and pepper may be added to taste. Serve several thin hot beef slices in your favorite buns with small bowls of beef juice for dunking. Makes 12 servings.

Would a coughing frog say he has a person in his throat?

HAMBURGERS

The most well-known and easiest snack to make to suit every taste. Everyone loves to build their own.

Lean ground beef	1 lb.	500 g
Dry bread crumbs	½ cup	125 mL
Water or milk	½ cup	125 mL
Salt	1 tsp.	5 mL
Pepper	¼ tsp.	1 mL
Worcestershire sauce (optional)	1 tsp.	5 mL
Chopped onion (optional)	⅓ cup	75 mL
Relish, ketchup and onion for garnish		
Hamburger buns, split and buttered	4 - 6	4 - 6

Put first 7 ingredients into bowl and mix. Shape into 4 large or 6 average size patties. Fry or barbecue.

Serve with relish, ketchup and onion on hamburger buns. Makes 4 to 6 burgers.

Note: Bread crumbs help to keep lean meat soft and moist. Quantity of crumbs and water may be cut in half if desired or left out entirely.

CHEESEBURGER: Put cheese slice on top of meat during last ½ minute of frying.

ITALIAN BURGER: Put mozzarella cheese slice on top of meat during last ½ minute of frying. Parmesan cheese may be added to meat mixture, about ⅓ cup (75 mL).

MUSHROOM BURGER: Add sliced mushrooms, fried. Some condensed mushroom soup can be mixed with mushrooms if preferred. Put on bun or on meat in bun.

AVOCADO BURGER: Put sliced avocado on top of meat in bun.

LOADED BURGER: To cheeseburger add fried Canadian bacon, tomato slice, pickles or relish, lettuce, mayonnaise.

Burger Options: Sliced white or purple onion, raw or fried, ketchup, mustard, relish, mayonnaise, pickles.

Note: An egg may be used to bind ingredients, although it makes a firmer patty when cooked. Use egg to bind when barbecuing.

CHICKENBURGERS

A pleasant change, these are delicious and different from everyday fare.

Boneless raw chicken, ground	1 lb.	450 g
Dry bread crumbs	¼ cup	50 mL
Milk or water	¼ cup	50 mL
Salt	1 tsp.	5 mL
Pepper	¼ tsp.	1 mL

Hamburger buns, split and buttered
Cranberry sauce
Ketchup

Mix all together in bowl. Shape into 4 large patties or 5 or 6 smaller ones. Fry in well greased pan. Put on buns. Serve with cranberry sauce or ketchup or both. Makes 4 to 6.

Note: These are also excellent with a fried bacon slice, avocado, tomato, mayonnaise and alfalfa sprouts added.

BACON AND EGG SANDWICH

A meal in a sandwich. Good without the egg too.

Egg, firmly fried	1	1
Salt and pepper sprinkle		
Bacon slices, cooked, halved	2 - 3	2 - 3
Toast slices, buttered	2	2
Ketchup (optional)		

Layer egg, salt, pepper and bacon between toast slices. Serve hot. Ketchup is optional. Makes 1.

BACON AND TOMATO SANDWICH: Omit egg. Add sliced tomato. Sprinkle with salt and pepper. A popular sandwich.

AVOCADO BACON SNACK: Add sliced avocado to Bacon and Tomato Sandwich.

BROILED FRENCH LOAF

Cut large chunks from this meaty, pizza flavored loaf as needed. Simple to make.

Lean ground beef	1 lb.	500 g
Chopped onion	½ cup	125 mL
Tomato sauce	7½ oz.	213 mL
Oregano	1 tsp.	5 mL
Salt	1 tsp.	5 mL
Pepper	½ tsp.	2 mL
Sweet basil	½ tsp.	2 mL
French loaf, split (or 3 submarine buns)	1	1
Parmesan cheese, grated		
Mozzarella cheese, grated		

Scramble-fry ground beef and onion until cooked.

Add next 5 ingredients. Heat through.

Spread over bread surface. Sprinkle with Parmesan cheese. Sprinkle thick layer Mozzarella down center of loaf. Broil 5 or 6 inches (12 or 15 cm) from heat. Makes about 3½ cups (800 mL) of filling.

BENEDICT BUN

Bacon, egg and cheese — they are all here — eggs benedict in a sandwich.

English muffin, split, toasted and buttered	1	1
Canadian bacon slice, fried	1	1
Egg, fried fairly hard	1	1
Salt and pepper sprinkle		
Processed cheese spread		

On bottom half of muffin, layer bacon and egg. Sprinkle with salt and pepper. Spread cheese on top muffin half and place over egg. Serve hot. Makes 1.

Throughout this book measurements are given in Conventional and Metric measure. To compensate for differences between the two measurements due to rounding, a full metric measure is not always used. The cup used is the standard 8 fluid ounce. Temperature is given in degrees Fahrenheit and Celsius. Baking pan measurements are in inches and centimetres as well as quarts and litres. An exact metric conversion is given below as well as the working equivalent (Standard Measure).

OVEN TEMPERATURES

Fahrenheit (°F)	Celsius (°C)
175°	80°
200°	95°
225°	110°
250°	120°
275°	140°
300°	150°
325°	160°
350°	175°
375°	190°
400°	205°
425°	220°
450°	230°
475°	240°
500°	260°

SPOONS

Conventional Measure	Metric Exact Conversion Millilitre (mL)	Metric Standard Measure Millilitre (mL)
$1/8$ teaspoon (tsp.)	0.6 mL	0.5 mL
$1/4$ teaspoon (tsp.)	1.2 mL	1 mL
$1/2$ teaspoon (tsp.)	2.4 mL	2 mL
1 teaspoon (tsp.)	4.7 mL	5 mL
2 teaspoons (tsp.)	9.4 mL	10 mL
1 tablespoon (tbsp.)	14.2 mL	15 mL

CUPS

	Metric Exact Conversion	Metric Standard Measure
$1/4$ cup (4 tbsp.)	56.8 mL	60 mL
$1/3$ cup ($5^1/3$ tbsp.)	75.6 mL	75 mL
$1/2$ cup (8 tbsp.)	113.7 mL	125 mL
$2/3$ cup ($10^2/3$ tbsp.)	151.2 mL	150 mL
$3/4$ cup (12 tbsp.)	170.5 mL	175 mL
1 cup (16 tbsp.)	227.3 mL	250 mL
$4^1/2$ cups	1022.9 mL	1000 mL (1 L)

PANS

Conventional Inches	Metric Centimetres
8x8 inch	20x20 cm
9x9 inch	22x22 cm
9x13 inch	22x33 cm
10x15 inch	25x38 cm
11x17 inch	28x43 cm
8x2 inch round	20x5 cm
9x2 inch round	22x5 cm
10x4$1/2$ inch tube	25x11 cm
8x4x3 inch loaf	20x10x7.5 cm
9x5x3 inch loaf	22x12.5x7.5 cm

DRY MEASUREMENTS

Conventional Measure Ounces (oz.)	Metric Exact Conversion Grams (g)	Metric Standard Measure Grams (g)
1 oz.	28.3 g	27 g
2 oz.	56.7 g	57 g
3 oz.	85.0 g	85 g
4 oz.	113.4 g	125 g
5 oz.	141.7 g	140 g
6 oz.	170.1 g	170 g
7 oz.	198.4 g	200 g
8 oz.	226.8 g	250 g
16 oz.	453.6 g	500 g
32 oz.	907.2 g	1000 g (1 kg)

CASSEROLES (Canada & Britain)

Standard Size Casserole	Exact Metric Measure
1 qt. (5 cups)	1.13 L
$1^1/2$ qts. ($7^1/2$ cups)	1.69 L
2 qts. (10 cups)	2.25 L
$2^1/2$ qts. ($12^1/2$ cups)	2.81 L
3 qts. (15 cups)	3.38 L
4 qts. (20 cups)	4.5 L
5 qts. (25 cups)	5.63 L

CASSEROLES (United States)

Standard Size Casserole	Exact Metric Measure
1 qt. (4 cups)	900 mL
$1^1/2$ qts. (6 cups)	1.35 L
2 qts. (8 cups)	1.8 L
$2^1/2$ qts. (10 cups)	2.25 L
3 qts. (12 cups)	2.7 L
4 qts. (16 cups)	3.6 L
5 qts. (20 cups)	4.5 L

SANDWICHES

SANDWICHES

SANDWICHES

SANDWICHES

Company's Coming cookbooks are available at retail locations throughout Canada!

EXCLUSIVE mail order offer on next page

Buy any 2 cookbooks—choose a 3rd FREE of equal or less value than the lowest price paid.

Original Series — CA$14.99 Canada — US$10.99 USA & International

CODE		CODE		CODE	
SQ	150 Delicious Squares	KC	Kids Cooking	FD	Fondues
CA	Casseroles	CT	Cooking For Two	CCBE	The Beef Book
MU	Muffins & More	BB	Breakfasts & Brunches	ASI	Asian Cooking
SA	Salads	SC	Slow Cooker Recipes	CB	The Cheese Book
AP	Appetizers	ODM	One-Dish Meals	RC	The Rookie Cook
DE	Desserts	ST	Starters	RHR	Rush-Hour Recipes
SS	Soups & Sandwiches	SF	Stir-Fry	SW	Sweet Cravings
CO	Cookies	MAM	Make-Ahead Meals	YRG	Year-Round Grilling **NEW** *March 1/03*
PA	Pasta	PB	The Potato Book		
BA	Barbecues	CCLFC	Low-Fat Cooking		
LR	Light Recipes	CCLFP	Low-Fat Pasta		
PR	Preserves	CFK	Cook For Kids		
CH	Chicken, Etc.	SCH	Stews, Chilies & Chowders		

Greatest Hits Series

CODE	CA$12.99 Canada US$9.99 USA & International
ITAL	Italian
MEX	Mexican

Lifestyle Series

CODE	CA$16.99 Canada US$12.99 USA & International
GR	Grilling
DC	Diabetic Cooking

CODE	CA$19.99 Canada US$17.99 USA & International
HC	Heart-Friendly Cooking **NEW** *Feb 1/03*

Special Occasion Series

CODE	CA$19.99 Canada US$17.99 USA & International
GFK	Gifts from the Kitchen
CFS	Cooking for the Seasons

CODE	CA$22.99 Canada US$17.99 USA & International
WC	Weekend Cooking **NEW** April 1/03

CODE	CA$24.99 Canada US$19.99 USA & International
HFH	Home for the Holidays

Company's Coming COOKBOOKS

COMPANY'S COMING PUBLISHING LIMITED
2311 – 96 Street
Edmonton, Alberta, Canada T6N 1G3
Tel: (780) 450-6223 Fax: (780) 450-1857
www.companyscoming.com

EXCLUSIVE Mail Order Offer

See previous page for list of cookbooks

Buy 2 Get 1 FREE!

Buy any 2 cookbooks—choose a **3rd FREE** of equal or less value than the lowest price paid.

Quantity	Code	Title	Price Each	Price Total
			$	$
		DON'T FORGET		
		to indicate your		
		FREE BOOK(S).		
		(see exclusive mail order		
		offer above)		
		please print		
	TOTAL BOOKS (including FREE)	**TOTAL BOOKS PURCHASED:**	$	

	International	Canada & USA
Plus Shipping & Handling (per destination)	$7.00 (one book)	$5.00 (1-3 books)
Additional Books (including FREE books)	$ ($2.00 each)	$ ($1.00 each)
Sub-Total	$	$
Canadian residents add G.S.T.(7%)		$
TOTAL AMOUNT ENCLOSED	$	$

The Fine Print

- Orders outside Canada must be **PAID IN US FUNDS** by cheque or money order drawn on Canadian or US bank or by credit card.
- Make cheque or money order payable to: **COMPANY'S COMING PUBLISHING LIMITED**.
- Prices are expressed in Canadian dollars for Canada, US dollars for USA & International and are subject to change without prior notice.
- Orders are shipped surface mail. For courier rates, visit our web-site: **companyscoming.com** or contact us:
  Tel: (780) 450-6223 Fax: (780) 450-1857.
- Sorry, no C.O.D.'s.

Gift Giving

- Let us help you with your gift giving!
- We will send cookbooks directly to the recipients of your choice if you give us their names and addresses.
- Please specify the titles you wish to send to each person.
- If you would like to include your personal note or card, we will be pleased to enclose it with your gift order.
- Company's Coming cookbooks make excellent gifts: birthdays, bridal showers, Mother's Day, Father's Day, graduation or any occasion ...collect them all!

☐ MasterCard ☐ VISA

Expiry date _____

Account # _____

Name of cardholder _____

Cardholder's signature _____

Shipping Address
Send the cookbooks listed above to:

Name: _____

Street: _____

City: _____ Prov./State: _____

Country: _____ Postal Code/Zip: _____

Tel: (___) _____

E-mail address: _____

☐ YES! Please send a catalogue

The weekend is finally here—time to relax with family, friends and plenty of good food! Keep the festivities rolling with your choice of casual entertaining ideas from *Weekend Cooking*.

Inside you'll find 40 creative menu plans featuring more than 200 all-new, kitchen-tested recipes. *Weekend Cooking* features everything from a laid-back video night of snacking to an exotic African safari party to a spicy Australian barbecue. Each recipe has been beautifully photographed and is easy to follow, for winning results every time.

Whenever family and friends come together on the weekend, save time to enjoy their company. Count on *Weekend Cooking* for your menu plan!

COOKBOOKS

Quick
&
Easy
Recipes

Everyday
Ingredients

Canada's
most popular
cookbooks!